GW00602061

Functional Mathematics

Bob Hartman

Victoria Kaye

Joan Knott

Graham Newman

Joe Petran

Julia Staves

Kevin Tanner

Series editor: Graham Newman

CAMBRIDGE UNIVERSITY PRESS
Cambridge, New York, Melbourne, Madrid, Cape Town, Singapore,
São Paulo, Delhi, Dubai, Tokyo

Cambridge University Press
The Edinburgh Building, Cambridge CB2 8RU, UK

www.cambridge.org
Information on this title: www.cambridge.org/9780521147125

© Cambridge University Press 2009

First published 2009

Book printed in the United Kingdom at the University Press, Cambridge

A catalogue record for this publication is available from the British Library

ISBN 978-0-521-14712-5 Paperback with CD-ROM for Windows and Mac

Cambridge University Press has no responsibility for the persistence or
accuracy of URLs for external or third-party internet websites referred to in
this publication, and does not guarantee that any content on such websites is,
or will remain, accurate or appropriate. Information regarding prices, travel
timetables and other factual information given in this work are correct at
the time of first printing but Cambridge University Press does not guarantee
the accuracy of such information thereafter.

NOTICE TO TEACHERS
It is illegal to reproduce any part of this book in material
form (including photocopying and electronic storage)
except under the following circumstances:
(i) where you are abiding by a licence granted to your
school or institution by the Copyright Licensing
Agency;
(ii) where no such licence exists, or where you wish to
exceed the terms of a licence, and you have gained
the written permission of Cambridge University
Press;
(iii) where you are allowed to reproduce without
permission under the provisions of Chapter 3 of
the Copyright, Designs and Patents Act 1988,
which covers, for example, the reproduction of
short passages within certain types of educational
anthology and reproduction for the purposes of
setting examination questions.

The CD-ROM at the back of this book is provided on
the following terms and conditions:
• The CD-ROM is made available for the use of
current teachers and students within a purchasing
institution, or for private purchasers, only. A
purchase of at least one copy of the book must be
made in respect of each teacher, student or private
purchaser who uses the CD-ROM. The CD-ROM
may be installed on individual computers or
networks for use as above.

• Subject to the above, the material on the CD-
ROM, in whole or in part, may not be passed in
an electronic form to another party, and may not
be copied (except for making one copy of the CD-
ROM solely for backup or archival purposes),
distributed, printed or stored electronically. It may
not be posted on a public website, and may not be
altered for any reason without the permission of
Cambridge University Press.
• Permission is explicitly granted for use of
the materials on a data projector, interactive
whiteboard or other public display in the context
of classroom teaching at a purchasing institution.
• Once a teacher or student ceases to be a member of
the purchasing institution all copies of the material
on the CD-ROM stored on his/her personal
computer must be destroyed and the CD-ROM
returned to the purchasing institution.
• All material contained within the CD-ROM is
protected by copyright and other intellectual
property laws. You may not alter, remove or destroy
any copyright notice or other material placed on or
with this CD-ROM.
• The CD-ROM is supplied 'as-is' with no express
guarantee as to its suitability.

Contents

The contents of this book and CD-ROM are copyright Cambridge University Press 2009

This book has been written to give students practice at applying mathematical skills to functional problems. It does not attempt to teach. There are many existing books on the market (for example, mathematics course books) that you can use to learn and practise mathematical skills, and to prepare for examinations and other assessments, such as key stage tests, GCSE or other vocational assessments. This book gives you some opportunities to use your skills to solve problems that are 'functional' in nature.

'Functional skills' is not a topic, but a process. It is not related to content, but to methods of solution and application, usually within a real-life context. Within this book contexts have been chosen around which questions and tasks have been written. These are just a sample of the many situations and contexts that we could have chosen from the rich variety of our everyday lives. It should not matter whether you are familiar with the contexts chosen, nor should it matter whether these contexts match your own areas of study. In learning to apply your mathematical knowledge as part of functional work, you will be learning skills that are transferable to other contexts. It is the nature of the problem solving that is important, not necessarily the context.

Functional skills focuses on the process by which problems are solved. These process skills are many and varied but can be grouped together under three separate headings.

Representing

- Making sense of situations and representing them
- Recognising that a situation can be represented using mathematics
- Making initial models of a situation using suitable forms of representation
- Deciding the methods of solution – what needs to be worked out, and what mathematical tools are needed to help
- Selecting the information to use

Analysing

- Processing and using mathematics
- Using appropriate mathematical procedures
- Examining patterns and relationships
- Changing values to see the effects on the outcome
- Finding results and solutions

Interpreting

- Interpreting and communicating the results of an analysis
- Drawing conclusions in the light of the situation
- Considering the appropriateness and accuracy of the solutions
- Choosing language and forms of presentation to communicate the results

Here is an example to illustrate some of these skills.

Holiday Cottage

The table below shows the temperatures and rainfall of four towns in Turkey over a period of 12 months.

The temperature is given in degrees Celsius, the rainfall in millimetres.

	J	F	M	A	M	J	J	A	S	O	N	D
Antalya												
Temp	10	12	13	15	20	25	28	27	25	20	15	12
Rain	250	170	75	40	35	15	5	5	20	50	120	270
Istambul												
Temp	5	6	7	12	17	21	23	24	22	18	13	8
Rain	110	90	70	40	30	20	20	30	60	80	100	120
Izmir												
Temp	8	9	12	15	20	23	25	27	23	20	15	10
Rain	120	80	70	40	30	20	10	10	20	50	80	120
Samsun												
Temp	7	7	8	10	15	18	22	23	20	17	13	10
Rain	70	60	60	50	40	30	20	30	60	80	90	80

Jo wants to buy a cottage in Turkey, but is not sure in which region of Turkey to start looking.

Use the information in the table to make some recommendations that Jo can consider.

There are many different solutions to this problem. You have been given little guidance to help you, but you do know that you have to make some recommendations, and will have to use the information to make some comparisons.

There are many processes that you can use to work towards a solution for this problem. These processes are at the heart of functional skills. You will not need to use all such processes for a single problem, but the following illustrates how this problem relates to functional skills.

Representing

- Making sense of situations and representing them
  You will need to make comparisons between the four regions, for temperature and rainfall.

- Recognising that a situation can be represented using mathematics
  You should realise that to make valid comparisons you need to use mathematics to summarise some of the data, for example finding the mean temperature or rainfall for each of the four regions. You will be representing the situation using mathematics if you do this.
- Deciding the methods of solution – what needs to be worked out, and what mathematical tools are needed to help
  This is certainly needed for this problem. You will have to decide which mathematics, which presentation and which arguments to use for a particular region. To provide evidence for your recommendations you will need to choose what calculation to do.
- Selecting the information to use
  Which information will you use? You will have to decide whether to use temperature, rainfall, or both, and whether to use all the figures. You may then have to extract them from the table for calculation.

Analysing

- Processing and using mathematics
  You will need to perform calculations, such as finding the range or the mean of a set of data.
- Using appropriate mathematical procedures
  The calculations you choose to use should be appropriate and help you support a recommendation.
- Finding results and solutions
  You will need to calculate the mean and range, and find other solutions to help support any recommendations that you might make.

Interpreting

- Interpreting and communicating the results of an analysis
  Having worked out means, ranges, etc., you will need to make some comparison between them, interpreting your results as part of making a recommendation.
- Drawing conclusions in the light of the situation
  Your conclusion will support any recommendations that you make.
- Choosing language and forms of presentation to communicate the results
  Will you present some information in tables, in graphs? How well will you convey the results of your calculations to support any recommendations?

After working through this book, you should have the necessary skills to approach such an open-ended problem.

In working through this book, you will be faced with:

- problems set in real-life contexts
- problems in which you will first have to decide upon the method of solution
- routine and non-routine problems
- situations where you have to apply your mathematical skills
- problems in which your technical knowledge of mathematics is tested
- problems that are practically based
- open-ended problems which may have more than one solution
- situations that are unfamiliar and that will require you to think independently.

All the questions and tasks in this book have been written to cover the level 2 content of functional skills. However, there is much here that is also assessed as part of the level 1 functional skills course, and will be useful to all students, whether they are aiming for a pass at level 1 or at level 2.

The questions and tasks are grouped by context, and within each group you will find problems of varying difficulty and requiring different processes of solution. These match real life in which you have to decide to take a course of action yourself towards finding solutions to problems that might come your way.

Each unit in the book shows how mathematics can be applied within a real-life context. As you work through the questions you will build up the necessary mathematical skills needed as part of functional skills. Towards the end of each unit the questions are more open-ended and task-based, similar to the questions that you may experience on functional skills examination papers.

When you have worked through this book, you will have increased your ability to deal with new situations and tasks. You will be better prepared to use mathematics in real-life contexts and to solve functional problems that come your way, in whatever field of employment you may be working.

Entertainment

1   The table shows the top ten TV programmes for one week.

Programme	Viewers – Week 27th October 2008	Change from previous week
Emmerdale (Fri)	992 779	−2
Who Do You Think You Are?	990 997	−2
Emmerdale (Mon)	3 000 987	
Coronation Street (Fri)	4.2 million	−1
EastEnders (Thu)	2.9 million	+2
Coronation Street (Wed)	3 008 890	+4
EastEnders (Mon)	3 997 678	
Coronation Street (Mon)	4 345 567	+3
EastEnders (Fri)	2.94 million	−4
The X Factor	4.9 million	

The number in the Change column shows the change in position from the previous week.

(a) Explain what it means when there is no number next to a programme.

(b) Draw a table showing the position of the programmes for the week of 27th October and then the previous week.

(c) In another week, the X Factor was watched by 9.96 million viewers. Write this number in figures.

(d) During Christmas week 33 736 900 people watched Coronation Street altogether, in the ratio 2 . 3 . 5 (Monday : Wednesday : Friday).
Calculate how many people watched Coronation Street on Monday, Wednesday and Friday.

2 This is a rule for working out an estimate of the cost in pounds of advertising in a newspaper. Lengths should be in millimetres.

> Advert cost = Width × Height ÷ 120 (Round to the nearest £)

(a) Calculate the estimate of the cost of an advert of size:

   (i) 133 mm by 195 mm

  (ii) 65 mm by 195 mm

 (iii) 133 mm by 96 mm

(b) The cost of an advert has been estimated as £270. The width of the advert is 167 mm. What is the height? Give your answer to the nearest millimetre.

(c) The cost of an advert has been estimated as £189. The height of the advert is 96 mm. What is the width? Give your answer to the nearest millimetre.

(d) The table below shows the standard column width for advertisements.

Hint

Column	1	2	3	4	5	6	7	8
Width (mm)	31	65	99	133	167	201	235	269

What is the width of the margin between each column on the page?

3 This table shows the total annual advertising expenditure by sectors of the media. The figures represent millions of pounds.

	2003	2004	2005	2006
Printed material	8359	8742	8581	8346
Television	4378	4652	4820	4594
Direct mail	2467	2449	2371	2322
Outdoor and transport	914	986	1043	1084
Radio	584	606	579	534
Cinema	180	192	188	188
Internet	465	825	1367	2016

(a) What was the total advertising expenditure in 2006?

(b) What was the mean annual expenditure for television?

(c) For which media sector has the expenditure fallen each year over the four years?

(d) Which media sector has had the greatest increase in expenditure?

4 These pie charts show the viewing share of the five terrestrial television channels during July and August.

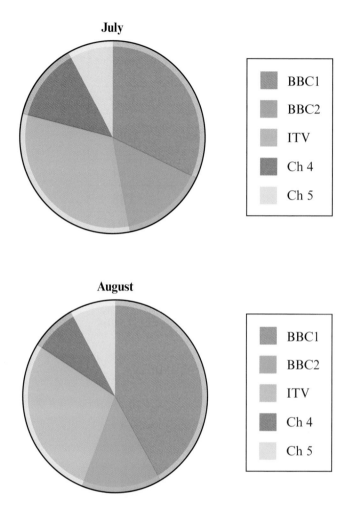

July

BBC1	
BBC2	
ITV	
Ch 4	
Ch 5	

August

BBC1	
BBC2	
ITV	
Ch 4	
Ch 5	

(a) Which two channels had a similar viewing share in August?

(b) Which two channels had a similar viewing share in July?

(c) Which channel did not change its viewing share from July to August?

(d) Which channel had the greatest change in viewing share from July to August?

(e) Overall, which is the most watched channel?

(f) It would be wrong to say that Channel 5 had the same viewing figures both months. Explain why.

5 An outside event is to be covered by two cameras, from 08 00 to 22 00. The diagram below shows a time plan for the two cameras.

	8	9	10	11	12	13	14	15	16	17	18	19	20	21	22
Camera 1															
Camera 2															

Avril, Ben, Charlie and Dave are four camera operators.

Each camera operator works two shifts during the day, which should total exactly 7 hours. They must have no more than 4 hours between each shift.

Copy the time plan for the two cameras, and show how you would allocate the four camera operators to these two cameras during the day.

6 (a) A page of a comic book measures 6 inches by 8 inches.
The title is a box that measures 5 inches by 2 inches.

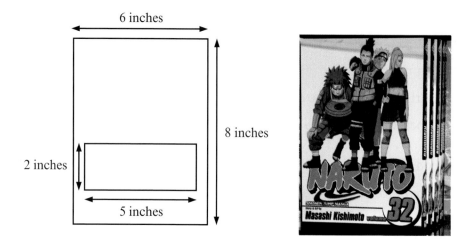

Use the conversion graph to convert these measurements to centimetres.

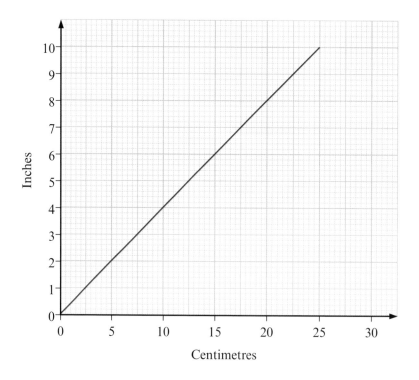

(b) A different comic book has dimensions 15 cm by 20 cm.

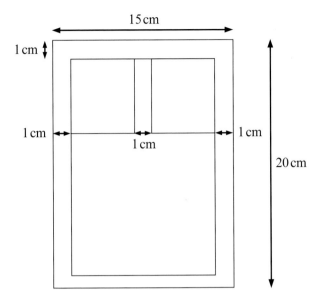

An artist wants to put six drawings on a page.

There must be a margin of 1 cm around the edge of the page, and at least 1 cm space between each drawing.

The six numbered drawings and the dimensions of each are shown below.

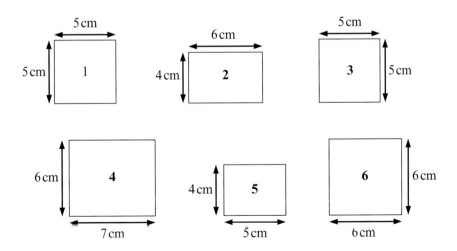

The drawings need to be arranged in order.

Will the drawings fit on the page?
Show calculations to justify your answer.

Hint

7 (a)

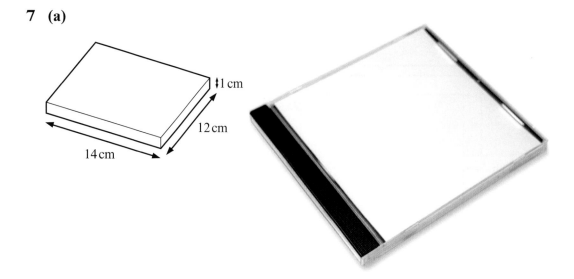

This diagram shows the dimensions of a CD case.

A box is needed for the CD case.

Draw a net of the box, using a scale of 1 : 2 (half size).

(b) The CDs are to be sold to a store for £10.50 each.
How many can be bought for £100?

(c) How much change should the shop have out of £100?

(d) The shop will sell the CD with VAT added. VAT is $17\frac{1}{2}$%.

How much VAT will need to be added to a CD costing £10.50?

(e) What will be the total cost of the CD with the VAT added?

The CD has a diameter of 12 cm.

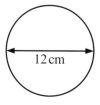

12 cm

(f) Use the formula $A = \pi \times r \times r$ to calculate the area A of the
CD. Take π to be 3.14, and r is the radius.

Hint

(g) Use the formula $C = 2 \times \pi \times r$ to calculate the circumference
C of the CD.

8 A media company conducted a questionnaire to identify potential readers for a new magazine about regional events. They wanted to know how many males and females would purchase the magazine.

(a) Complete the tree diagram below to illustrate possible responses.

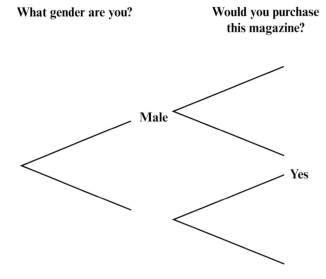

What gender are you?   **Would you purchase this magazine?**

Male

Yes

(b) The questionnaire was given to 40 males and 20 females. Thirty males said they would not buy the magazine, and 50% of females said they would. Based on this information the company concludes the magazine is equally likely to sell to males and females. Explain why this statement is incorrect.

(c) It is calculated that 20% of the UK population subscribes to a magazine. What is the probability that a person stopped at random in the UK does not subscribe to a magazine?

(d) A questionnaire asked the following questions:

What is your gender (male or female)?

What is your age (below 20, 20–50 or above 50)?

Do you drive a car (yes or no)?

Show all the possible responses on a tree diagram.

9 Chapter One

Make sure you write down all of your working and answers clearly.

Chapter One is a boy band. They are about to release their second album. As the assistant to the band you have been asked to coordinate the concert dates and venues.

The Main Street venue is illustrated here. (not to scale).

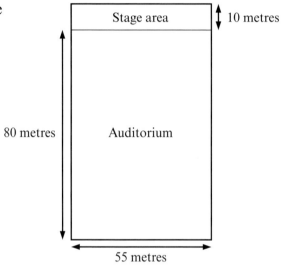

It is the venue's policy to allow each person 1.5 m^2 of standing space in the auditorium – this includes the security staff.

It takes one security staff member 30 seconds to check each person and admit them into the venue.

For every 100 customers there must be one member of security.

Each member of the security team costs £100 per night.

The stage area is not to be included in the calculations.

You must decide on the maximum number of tickets you can offer, and what time to open the venue doors so that everyone is in and the concert can start at 8 p.m.

The Clothes Shop

1 David & Claire is a retail shop selling fashion clothes for men and women.

David needs to arrange a number of clothes rails on the shop floor.
Each clothes rail takes up a rectangular area of the floor of dimensions 3 m by 1 m.

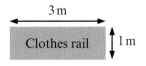

(a) Work out the greatest number of clothes rails that David can arrange on the shop floor, which is in the shape of a rectangle of dimensions 13 m by 10 m.

Hint

There must always be at least one metre of space around each clothes rail and at least two metres between clothes rails. Show your arrangement in a diagram.

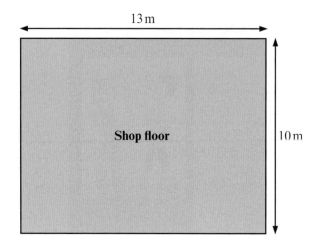

A maximum of 30 items can be hung on each clothes rail.
An order of 150 dresses, 90 blouses, 120 jackets and 270 pairs of trousers has just been delivered. One clothes rail is to be filled with dresses, one with blouses, one with jackets and one with trousers.

(b) **(i)** What fraction of the 150 dresses are put on a clothes rail?

(ii) What fraction of the 120 jackets will **not** be put on a clothes rail?

(c) How many more clothes rails would be needed to hang all of these clothes?

2 The delivery of clothes in question **1** arrived in some boxes.

Angela unpacks $\frac{1}{2}$ of the boxes. Mason unpacks $\frac{2}{5}$ of the boxes.

Emma unpacks the remaining boxes.

(a) What fraction of the boxes does Emma unpack?

(b) If Mason unpacks 20 boxes, how many boxes were delivered?

Hint

(c) Angela thinks 21 boxes were delivered. If everyone only unpacked whole boxes, why is she incorrect?

Each box is a cuboid with dimensions 1 m by 0.8 m by 0.6 m.
The boxes come in crates with dimensions 8 m by 3 m by 3.6 m.

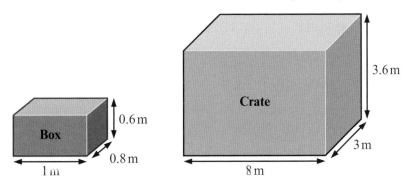

(d) Work out the greatest number of boxes that can fit into one crate.

The delivery company would like to use crates large enough to hold 250 boxes.

(e) Design a crate that could be used to hold up to 250 boxes.

3 David & Claire employ nine staff: five men and four women. The men work in the Men's department and the women work in the Women's department. They each have a one-hour lunch break which must be taken between 12 00 and 14 00. The diagram shows the lunch break rota.

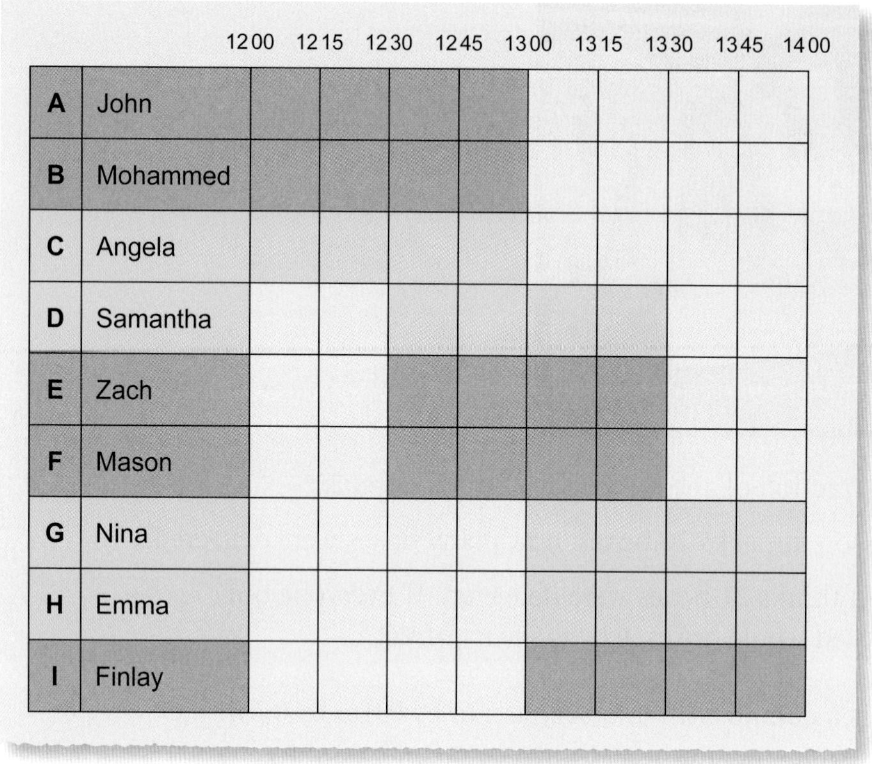

		1200	1215	1230	1245	1300	1315	1330	1345	1400
A	John	▓	▓	▓	▓					
B	Mohammed	▓	▓	▓						
C	Angela		▓	▓	▓					
D	Samantha			▓	▓	▓				
E	Zach		▓	▓	▓					
F	Mason				▓	▓	▓			
G	Nina					▓	▓	▓		
H	Emma					▓	▓	▓		
I	Finlay					▓	▓	▓	▓	

(a) Which staff are at lunch at: **(i)** 12 20 **(ii)** 13 40?

(b) How many men are on lunch between 12 30 and 13 00?

(c) How many women are working between 13 00 and 13 30?

Claire says that there must be at least two women and at least two men working in the shop at all times.

(d) Change the above lunch rota to ensure that there are at least two women and at least two men working in the shop at all times.

Hint

4 The diagrams are of print-outs from the tills in each department, showing the sales made on one day from 13 00 to 14 00.

Each member of staff is shown on the print-out with a letter showing each individual sale.

For example,

A ……… £17.99 shows that John made a sale of £17.99,

B ……… £24.50 shows that Mohammed made a sale of £24.50.

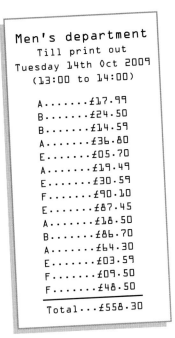

```
Men's department
   Till print out
Tuesday 14th Oct 2009
   (13:00 to 14:00)

   A.......£17.99
   B.......£24.50
   B.......£14.59
   A.......£36.80
   E.......£05.70
   A.......£19.49
   E.......£30.59
   F.......£90.10
   E.......£87.45
   A.......£18.50
   B.......£86.70
   A.......£64.30
   E.......£03.59
   F.......£09.50
   F.......£48.50

Total...£558.30
```

```
Women's department
   Till print out
Tuesday 14th Oct 2009
   (13:00 to 14:00)

   C.......£08.79
   C.......£53.79
   D.......£63.89
   C.......£39.55
   C.......£22.89
   D.......£86.99
   D.......£43.00

Total...£318.90
```

A	John
B	Mohammed
C	Angela
D	Samantha
E	Zach
F	Mason
G	Nina
H	Emma
I	Finlay

(a) Who made the greatest number of sales?

Hint

(b) Who took the greatest amount of money?

(c) Calculate the mean sale for the men's department and for the women's department. Comment on these results.

Hint

(d) Each staff member is paid commission at a rate of 2 per cent of the money they take for each sale. How much commission is Samantha paid for her sales between 13 00 and 14 00 on this day? Give your answer correct to the nearest penny.

(e) Work out the amount taken by Zach and Mason as a percentage of the total takings for the men's department. Give your answer to the nearest one per cent.

5 The pie charts show the percentage of sales in each of the departments for October and November.

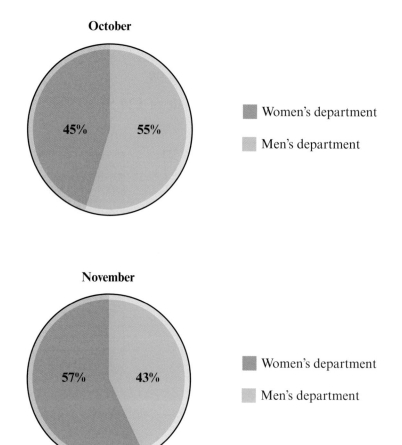

October

45% 55%

■ Women's department

□ Men's department

November

57% 43%

■ Women's department

□ Men's department

(a) Half of the total sales in the men's department in October were accessories. What percentage of the overall October sales were not men's accessories?

(b) Claire says that over these two months the women's department has taken more money than the men's department.

Give an example to show that this may not be true.

Hint

6 In the men's department, Finlay has 54 T-shirts to sell in a sale. The normal price of each T-shirt is £12.

(a) How much money would be taken if Finlay sold all of these T-shirts for £12 each?

David tells Finlay that, in the sale, his target is £500 for selling all 54 T-shirts. Finlay decides upon a special offer for selling these T-shirts. The special offer is:

'Buy one T-shirt for £12 and get the second at half price'.

(b) Finlay sells all of the T-shirts. Does he make his target? You must explain your answer fully.

Hint

SALE

Buy one for £12 and get the 2nd at $\frac{1}{2}$ price

(c) Describe a better offer that Finlay could have used to sell these T-shirts and meet his target of £500.

Hint

In the women's department sale, Nina has 12 dresses to sell. The normal price of each dress is £39.55. Nina's target is £270.

(d) What is the lowest price in the sale each of these dresses can be if Nina is to meet her target?

(e) In the sale, Nina sells the dresses for £29.99 each. How many dresses must she sell to meet her target?

7 The Men's Department

Make sure you write down all of your working and answers clearly.

These tables show the sales figures for men's clothing for the trading year 2007–08, by size and value and by size and quantity.

Men's sales (£)

	January	February	March	April	May	June
Small	25 000	23 555	30 250	12 531	30 000	32 000
Medium	75 005	72 005	100 021	36 024	96 000	99 021
Large	65 127	57 622	62 277	21 001	73 500	55 487
	July	**August**	**September**	**October**	**November**	**December**
Small	25 012	25 036	65 455	36 001	26 523	59 875
Medium	78 564	82 154	78 524	118 235	85 478	83 824
Large	55 077	61 007	89 565	92 329	67 734	95 799

Men's sales (quantities)

	January	February	March	April	May	June
Small	1000	800	1212	1239	1200	3960
Medium	2356	2954	4568	5465	3840	3960
Large	3510	3521	3351	3521	3521	2658
	July	**August**	**September**	**October**	**November**	**December**
Small	950	984	2654	1500	1060	2218
Medium	3142	3286	3140	4729	3419	3942
Large	3501	3541	2546	2399	2541	3000

Fifty-seven per cent of total store sales were in ladies' wear.

Ladies' garments are purchased in the ratio:
(Size 10–12 : Size 14–16 : Size 18–20) as (2 : 3 : 2).

(a) Suggest and justify the ratio in which men's garments should be purchased.

(b) Is there a trend in the the total quantity of items sold over the year?

(c) Construct a graph to illustrate sales (£) for the year. Comment on what your graph tells you.

(d) Which month do you think there was a sale and why?

Conservatories

1 Here are the floor plans of four conservatories.

(i)

2.7 m

3.8 m

(ii)

House wall

5.6 m

3.7 m

3.5 m

6.2 m

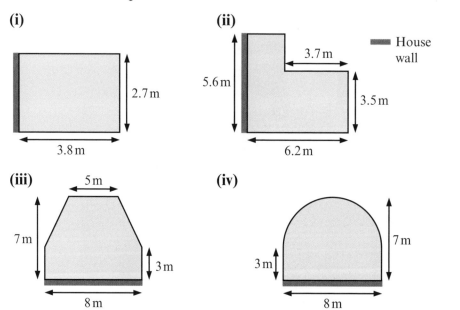

(iii)

5 m

7 m

3 m

8 m

Hint

(iv)

7 m

3 m

8 m

(a) Estimate the areas of these floor plans.

Show your workings.

(b) Work out the exact areas of the floor plans.

Hint

Hint

(c) The length of the plastics (plastic frames with window units inside) for conservatory **(iii)** is

3 m + 3 m + 5 m + 4.3 m + 4.3 m = 19.6 m.

This is the perimeter of the conservatory minus the length of the house wall. The house wall is shown in brown.

Find the length of plastics needed for the other conservatories.

Hint

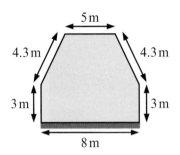

(d) On a grid, design an L-shaped conservatory that has an area of 29 m².

Hint

(e) A rectangular conservatory is built against the side of a house.

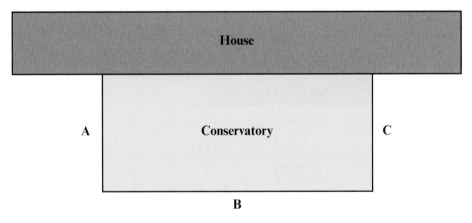

Sides **A**, **B** and **C** of the conservatory have a total length of 10 m.

What is the maximum area of the floor of the conservatory?

(f) Conservatories need a concrete base that is 100 mm thick. Find the volume of concrete needed for conservatories **(i)**, **(ii)**, **(iii)** and **(iv)**.

Hint

(g) Ready mixed concrete costs £95 per cubic metre (m³). There is a £25 delivery charge and VAT on the total cost. Calculate the cost of concrete for each of the four conservatories. Use a VAT rate of 17.5%.

2 Concrete is used to make foundations.
Concrete is made from cement, sand, gravel and water.
A common type of concrete used to make foundations for
conservatories is C20P concrete.

The table gives the weights of cement, sand and gravel needed to
make $1\,m^3$ of C20P concrete.

C20P concrete ($1\,m^3$)	Weight (kg)
Cement	300
Sand	600
Gravel	1200

(a) Write down the ratio of sand to gravel in C20P concrete.
Give your ratio in its simplest form.

(b) Write down the ratio of cement to aggregate (sand and
gravel) in C20P concrete. Give your ratio in its simplest form.

(c) Work out the weight of cement needed to make $1.75\,m^3$ of
C20P concrete.

A builder wants to make some C20P concrete.
He has $210\,kg$ of cement, $450\,kg$ of sand and $780\,kg$ of gravel.

(d) Work out the largest volume of concrete the builder can make.

Hint

3 Water is added to cement and aggregate to make concrete. The amount of water that should be added depends on the weight of the cement used.

The graph shows the volume of water needed for different weights of cement.

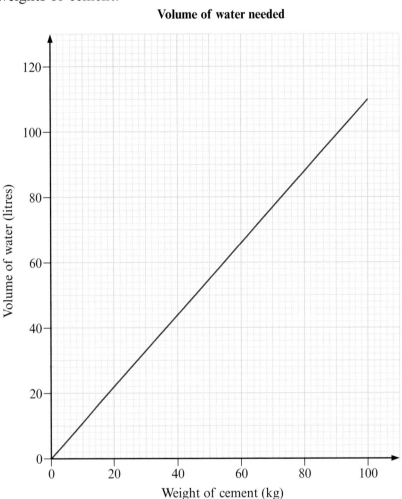

Volume of water needed

(a) Use the graph to estimate the volume of water needed for 50 kg of cement.

(b) The aggregate used to make concrete is seldom dry. Wet aggregate may contain as much as 0.05 litres of water per kilogram of aggregate.

A builder wants to make 1 m³ of C20P concrete using the quantities given in question **2**.

Comment on the volume of water the builder should add to make this concrete.

Hint

4 A concrete mixer is used to make concrete.

The table shows the hire charges for a concrete mixer at three different shops.

	1st day	Each additional day	Additional weekend (Sat, Sun)	All 5 weekdays (Mon–Fri)
U-Hire	£14	£10	£17.50	£48
Dylan's	£12.50	£12.50	£15	£50
Hire shop	£13.75	£11.50	£16.50	£52

A builder wants to hire a concrete mixer on a Monday for 3 days.

(a) Which shop should he use?

(b) Does it make any difference to your answer to part **(a)** if the concrete mixer is hired later in the week? Explain your answer.

(c) The hire charge listed does not include VAT of 17.5%.

Work out the VAT for these hire charges.

(i) £24   **(ii)** £38   **(iii)** £17.50

(d) A job is to lay 6.2 m³ of concrete. Calculate the expected cost of the job using **(i)** ready mix and **(ii)** self mix concrete. Comment on the costs.

Hint

> Concrete materials (self mix)   £75 per m³ (including VAT)
> Self mix labour £25 per m³
> Ready mix concrete £89 per m³ + £20 delivery + VAT
> Ready mix labour £17 per m³
> Concrete mixer (needed for 2 days)   £22 per day (including VAT)

5 Ms Brown wants to buy a conservatory. The conservatory costs £12 000. Here are some methods of buying the conservatory.

Method 1: 10% deposit plus monthly payments of £220 for 5 years

Method 2: 25% deposit plus monthly payments of £290 for 3 years

Method 3: Monthly payments of £125 for 10 years

Method 4: Pay £12 000 in full

Compare these methods of buying the conservatory.

6 The diagram shows the floor plan of a conservatory.
All the doors are the same width.

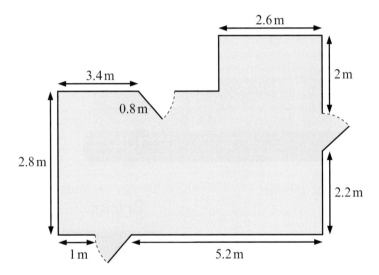

The table gives sizes of conservatory furniture.

Furniture	Width (cm)	Length (cm)
Settee	98	120
Small chair	60	79
Large chair	67	88
Small table	50	78
Large table	58	90

Draw a scale diagram to show how the conservatory furniture can sensibly be put into the conservatory.

7 Make a quote

Make sure you write down all of your working and answers clearly.

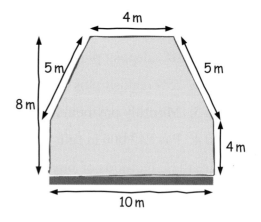

You have been asked to install the hexagonal conservatory shown in the sketch.

You will need to provide:

Concrete base 100 mm deep

Plastics for all walls (except the house wall, shown in brown in the sketch)

A wall to go below the plastics. This wall is 90 cm high. The length of wall is the length of the plastics less the 80 cm door. A builder has calculated you will need 15 packs of 200 bricks.

You will need these amounts of labour:

1 hour of general labour per 4 m² of floor plan for laying the concrete base

1 hour of building labour per 150 bricks for walling

2 hours of window fitting labour per 3 metres of plastics

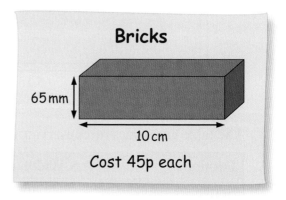

Bricks

65 mm

10 cm

Cost 45p each

Labour costs

General £11 per hour
Building £12.50 per hour
Window fitting £10 per hour

Building suppliers price list (including VAT)

Concrete   £92 per m³ + £30 delivery
Plastics   £275 per metre (including doors)

(a) Work out the cost of building this conservatory. Include all the costs for

    (i) concrete   **(ii)** walling   **(iii)** plastics

(b) Provide a quote for supplying this conservatory.
    Add 25% to the total cost for profit.

Hospitals

1 The Royal College of Nursing recommends that a hospital ward is staffed with at least 65% qualified nurses. The other staff are healthcare assistants.

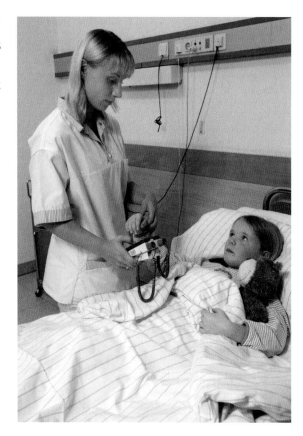

Jilly is the nurse manager of a ward.

(a) To help her work out a roster she needs answers to some questions. Write the answers to Jilly's questions.

   (i) What is the ratio of qualified nurses to healthcare assistants in its simplest form?

   (ii) What fraction of the staff must be qualified nurses?

(b) Jilly has 13 qualified nurses on the roster one day. How many healthcare assistants will she need if she has the minimum number of nurses required?

(c) If there is one healthcare assistant on the night shift, how many qualified nurses should be on duty?

2 The results of an NHS survey are shown in the table.

Hospital out-patients waiting times	
Less than 1 hour	30%
At least 1 hour but less than 2 hours	18%
At least 2 hours but less than 4 hours	24%
At least 4 hours but less than 8 hours	21%
8 hours or longer	7%

(a) Draw a pie chart to show this information for the monthly report.

The number of people who took part in the survey was 34 528.

(b) How many patients waited less than one hour?

(c) What is the probability of a patient being seen in less than two hours?

Hint

3 Nurses work an eight-hour shift. They may not work more than five hours without a one-hour meal/rest break. There must always be at least one nurse in the side room.

Hint

Anna's shift is shown in the diagram.

	08 00	10 00	12 00	14 00	16 00	18 00	20 00	22 00	24 00
Anna									

What is the minimum number of nurses working eight-hour shifts needed to staff the side room between 08 00 and midnight?

4 The table shows a group of patients who have been promised appointments next week, and the number of days for which they will need a hospital bed.

Mrs Jones	1	Miss Stevens	2
Miss Naidoo	5	Miss Khan	3
Mrs Green	3	Mrs Chang	4
Ms Smith	2		

Four beds are available from Monday to Friday.

Draw up a schedule to enable the hospital to give these patients their appointments.

5

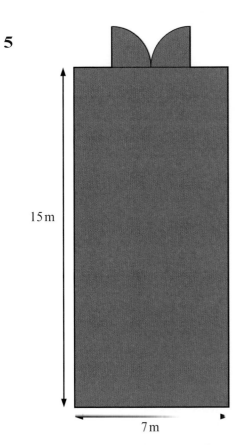

15 m

7 m

The diagram shows a small hospital ward 15 m long by 7 m wide with doors at one end.

A hospital bed is 6 ft long by $2\frac{1}{2}$ ft wide.

Draw a floor plan of the ward to show where the beds can be positioned if a gap at least 2 m wide is left between the beds.

Hint

6 Patients in Accident and Emergency departments at three hospitals were asked if they felt that the staff had done everything possible to control their pain whilst in the department. A summary of their replies is given in the tables.

St George's Hospital

Patients' replies	
Yes	2356
They could have done more	734
No	476
I was not in pain	434
Total patients surveyed	4000

St Mary's Hospital

Patients' replies	
Yes	2043
They could have done more	534
No	376
I was not in pain	547
Total patients surveyed	3500

The James Street Infirmary

Patients' replies	
Yes	1843
They could have done more	434
No	276
I was not in pain	447
Total patients surveyed	3000

St George's Hospital changes the responses into points for each hospital and therefore claims to have the best record.

'Yes', score **2** points
'They could have done more', score **−1** point
'No', score **−1** point
'I was not in pain', score **0** points.

(a) Use the information in the tables to investigate the claim.

Is this a valid way of comparing the performances of the three hospitals? Say why or why not.

(b) Find a different way of comparing the performances of the hospitals and see if you come to the same conclusion.

You must show your calculations and state how you have used them to get your answer.

7 Car Boot Sale

The Friends of the Children's Ward want to hold a car boot sale in the summer of 2009 to raise money for more toys for the ward. A planning committee with Cerys as the chairperson has been set up to organise the event.

To help them, Cerys has made a spreadsheet containing the weather records for the last few years and the car boot attendance figures for a similar event held 20 miles away.

Month: 4 = April, 5 = May, 6 = June, 7 = July
Temperatures are average monthly temperatures.

Rain is the total rainfall in millimetres that month.

Sunshine is the total number of hours of sunshine that month.

South Coast Weather

	A	B	C	D	E
	Year	Month	Temp (°C)	Rain (mm)	Sunshine (h)
1					
2	2003	4	13.4	27.2	208.0
3	2003	5	15.9	50.2	234.8
4	2003	6	19.8	41.6	256.0
5	2003	7	21.2	59.6	286.9
6					
7	2004	4	13.1	70.4	198.8
8	2004	5	16.1	40.4	254.4
9	2004	6	19.7	26.1	268.8
10	2004	7	19.8	37.2	235.3
11					
12	2005	4	12.7	49.1	181.0
13	2005	5	16.1	29.4	241.5
14	2005	6	19.8	27.3	270.9
15	2005	7	21	63.2	236.1
16					
17	2006	4	12.4	29	180.5
18	2006	5	15.6	64.3	200.6
19	2006	6	19.6	17.4	321.3
20	2006	7	23.9	24.4	335.3
21					
22	2007	4	17.1	1.6	273.8
23	2007	5	16.6	98.5	189.2
24	2007	6	19.5	68.9	198.8
25	2007	7	19.8	98.4	253.9
26					
27	2008	4	13.6	47.1	191.8
28	2008	5	18.9	90.4	244.0
29	2008	6	19.5	22.3	251.8
30	2008	7	20.9	40.3	226.2

Car boot sales figures (visitors paying on the gate) for similar events

Year	2002	2003	2005	2006	2008
Visitors	377	506	612	804	819

Use the information provided by Cerys to help you answer these questions. Make sure you write down all of your working and answers clearly.

If you make any assumptions or have any comments about your assumptions (or those of Cerys's committee!) jot them down clearly.

(a) Cerys used the information from similar events to estimate the number of visitors they could expect.

How many visitors do you think they should expect?
Show clearly how you estimated – don't just guess!

Hint

(b) People who sell at car boot sales need to rent a pitch from which to sell. This is an area of ground big enough for an average car, with room for a table, chair and perhaps a clothes rack.

    (i) Sketch a plan and estimate the size of a suitable pitch. Remember you want as many pitches as possible.

Hint

    (ii) It is planned to use one of a college's football fields for the car boot sale. The field measures about 90 m by 50 m. For health and safety reasons there must be a walkway of about 1 metre right round each pitch. There also needs to be a pathway, 2 m wide, for customers to walk between the rows of pitches. Make a rough, dimensioned sketch of the field using your pitch layout sizes. How many pitches can be fitted on the field?

The committee decide on the basic rules and regulations of the car boot sale:

> Cost £15 per pitch.
>
> For **SAFETY** reasons, stalls **must not** extend into the aisles. How you use your pitch area is up to you, but your whole stall, and your sales staff, **must** fit into this area. Extending into the aisles cannot be tolerated for safety reasons.
>
> We will open at 12.15 for setting up. The sale will begin at 1.30pm. Buyers pay 50p on the gate.

(c) The committee estimate that about 75% of the pitches will be rented.
Given this and your answer to part **(a)** estimate the total takings.

(d) The final decision the committee needs to take is when to hold the car boot sale.
It can be in April, May, June or July.
Use the weather records to decide which will be the best month in which to hold a car boot sale.
Use figures, calculations, graphs and charts to give evidence in support of your choice.

Rubbish

1 The table below shows the amount of rubbish in a hotel dustbin.

Material	Percentage of rubbish
Organic	35
Paper	30
Glass	7
Plastics	
Metal	6
Other	13

(a) What percentage of the rubbish was plastics?

The hotel uses bins containing 80 litres of rubbish.

(b) How many litres of metal do you expect one bin to contain?

(c) Draw a pie chart to show the information in the table.

The hotel begins to recycle by separating out the organics and paper into separate 80-litre bins.
The rest is placed in all-purpose dustbins and sent to landfill.
One week they produce 2000 litres of rubbish.

(d) How many bins will be collected for:

    (i) Paper?   (ii) Organics?   (iii) Landfill?

2 The Plaza Hotel considers four different companies to transport their rubbish to the tip.

Hint

Waste removal company	Cost
Waste Move	£17 per tonne
Easy Skip	£57.50 for each 5 tonne load
Skip Hire	£50 weekly plus £9 per tonne
Tip It	£112.75 per week for up to 10 tonnes

(a) Which firm should the hotel use if:

    (i) they produce 7 tonnes per week?

    (ii) they produce 15 tonnes per week?

(b) Comment on which firm is cheapest.

3 The dimensions of some recycling bins are shown below.

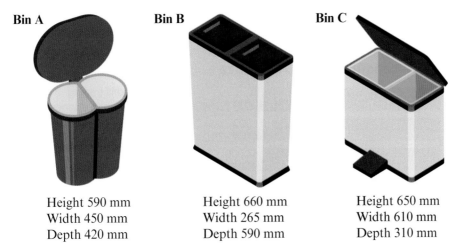

Bin A

Height 590 mm
Width 450 mm
Depth 420 mm

Bin B

Height 660 mm
Width 265 mm
Depth 590 mm

Bin C

Height 650 mm
Width 610 mm
Depth 310 mm

For delivery, the bins are placed in a cardboard carton.

Sheets of cardboard are available in the following sizes:

2070 × 1500 mm   1810 × 1500 mm   1410 × 1500 mm

(a) Make a scale drawing showing how the nets for each carton could be cut from the sheets of cardboard.

(b) Work out how much waste cardboard there is from each carton.

The diagram shows the plan of a kitchen.

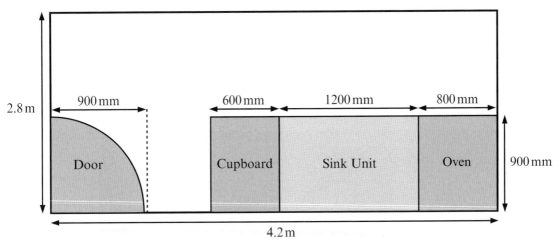

(c) Hamid wants to tile the kitchen floor.
He uses square tiles with side length 40 cm.

Hint

  (i) How many tiles will he need?

  (ii) How many pieces of tiles will be left over?
      Give the dimensions of each piece.

4 The chart shows the estimate made by one local authority for the amount of waste to be sent for landfill compared with their Landfill Trading Allowance.

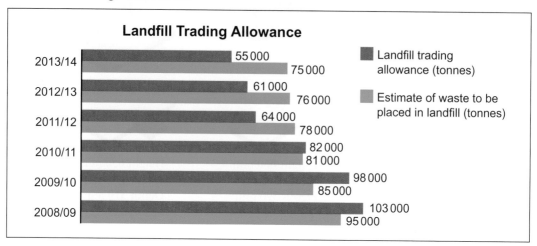

Landfill Trading Allowance

Year	Landfill trading allowance (tonnes)	Estimate of waste to be placed in landfill (tonnes)
2013/14	55 000	75 000
2012/13	61 000	76 000
2011/12	64 000	78 000
2010/11	82 000	81 000
2009/10	98 000	85 000
2008/09	103 000	95 000

(a) What is their allowance for 2011/2012?

Hint

If the local authority sends more waste for landfill than their allowance, they have to pay a fine. The fine is worked out using the formula:

$$F = 150(W - A)$$

where F is the fine in pounds, W is the waste put into landfill and A is the Landfill Trading Allowance.

(b) What should this authority expect to pay in fines in 2011/2012?

(c) In which year would the authority expect to pay a fine of £2 250 000?

(d) Copy and complete the table from the chart to show the amount of waste that exceeds the authority's allowances.

Hint

Year	Estimate of waste to be placed in landfill (tonnes)	Landfill Trading Allowance (tonnes)	Amount of waste exceeding the allowance (tonnes)
2008/09	95 000	103 000	−8000
2009/10	85 000	98 000	
2010/11			
2011/12			
2012/13			
2013/14	75 000	55 000	20 000
Totals			

The authority is allowed to bank its surplus allowances to use in later years.

(e) Use the formula above part **(b)** to work out how much the authority will pay in fines over these six years.

(f) Compare what happens to the amount of rubbish the authority expects to place in landfill with the allowances in the years from 2008 to 2014.

(g) Explain why it might be difficult for the authority to estimate how much it might have to pay in fines in 2016/17.

Of the 62 English local authorities, 28 need to buy additional allocations.

(h) What percentage of the English local authorities is this?

5 The table shows the shift patterns for four weeks in the Transport division for a local authority.

Drivers work five days on followed by three rest days.

Each shift is ten hours long including lunch and breaks.

	Week 1	Week 2	Week 3	Week 4
Mon	Jones	Jones	Jones	Jones
Tue	Jones	Jones	Jones	Jones
Wed		Jones	Jones	Jones
Thu			Jones	Jones
Fri				Jones
Sat	Jones			
Sun	Jones	Jones		

(a) Draw tables to show the shift patterns for the following drivers:

   (i) Knox begins his Week 1 shift on Monday

   (ii) Smith begins her Week 1 shift on Wednesday

   (iii) Bakir begins his Week 1 shift on Thursday

Bakir earns £8.50 per hour and is paid overtime at time and a quarter. He is paid for his lunch and breaks.

(b) What will be his gross pay in Week 3 if he works an additional ten-hour shift?

Hint

Bakir drives four loads to the recycling plant in an articulated lorry.

It carries 25 tonnes of rubbish. His lorry does 6 mpg.

Knox drives an eight-wheeled rigid lorry that carries 15 tonnes of rubbish.

He carries six loads per day. His lorry does 8 mpg.

It is 20 miles to the recycling plant from the tip.

(c) **(i)** How much fuel does Bakir use in a day?

   (ii) How much fuel does Knox use in a day?

(d) Which lorry carries the most rubbish per gallon?

Hint

6 The table shows the recycling rates for the nine regions in the UK for 2006/07.

Ranking in 2006/7	Region	Change
1	East	0
2	South West	1
3	East Midlands	−1
4	South East	0
5	North West	1
6	Yorkshire and the Humber	2
7	North East	0
8	London	1
9	West Midlands	−4

The Change column shows the change in the table from the previous year.

Draw a table to show the rankings for 2005/06.

7 Vending machine mania

Make sure you write down all of your working and answers clearly.

St Gill's School in Wales collected information about their use of vending machines and the rubbish resulting from them.

> **Information about the school**
>
> There are 750 students.
>
> There are 2 dining halls both about $500\,m^2$.
>
> Water is allowed in lessons, but nothing else.

Each vending machine holds 5 rows of drinks.

Each row has 9 slots across and is 8 slots deep.

This table summarises the costs of the different drinks sold, the profit per drink and whether or not the containers can be recycled.

Cost of drinks and their containers

Type of drink	Cost	Container	Profit
Spring water	50p	Plastic – not recyclable by school	5p
Milkshake – strawberry, banana or chocolate	£1.00	Plastic – not recyclable by school	10p
Milk	35p	Cardboard carton – recyclable	3p
Fresh juice – orange or apple	40p	Plastic – not recyclable by school	4p
Fresh juice – cranberry, orange, apple or pineapple	50p	Aluminium can – recyclable	5p (1p extra if can recycled)

This pie chart shows the results of a survey of the students' favourite drinks.

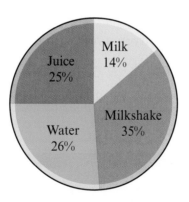

The school needs to reduce the cost of rubbish produced.

(a) Work out the capacity of the vending machine.

(b) Decide on how many of each type of drink you would use to fill the vending machine once it has been emptied.

Remember to consider the amount of rubbish created, the profit made and the student preference.

(c) What percentage of the containers in your vending machine can be recycled by the school?

(d) How much profit would be made?

Restaurants

1 The diagram shows the floor plan of a restaurant in a hotel.

Hint

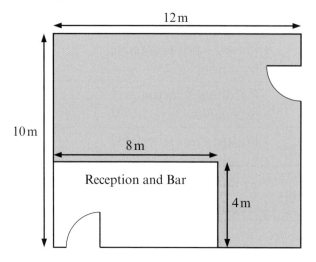

The hotel owner is carpeting the shaded area.

Carpet is sold by the metre from a roll with a choice of widths.

Width (metres)	2	3	4	5
Price per metre	£12.56	£18.50	£23.48	£27.05

Find the minimum cost of the carpet.

2 The hotel in question **1** uses two types of table in the restaurant.

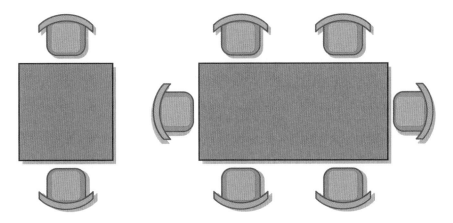

They have square tables which seat 2 people.
The sides of these tables are 900 mm in length.

They also have rectangular tables which seat 4–6 people and have a length of 1800 mm and a width of 900 mm.

There must be a gap of 1.4 m between tables and a gap of 1 m between tables and the wall to allow the staff to serve the customers.

(a) Make a scale drawing of the restaurant showing where you would place the tables to accommodate these people.

> Two couples
> Four groups of four people
> One group of five and one group of six people

Hint

(b) The restaurant is set up for a banquet by placing the tables end to end in long rows. One short end may be against a wall.

How many people could be seated at the banquet?

45

3 The chart shows the lunchtime bookings for six tables at Cosy For You restaurant.

Table	Seats	1100	1200	1300	1400	1500
1	4			Lewis (6)		
2	2			Lewis (6)		
3	4		Jones (4)			
4	2					
5	8					
6	4					

Bookings are usually made for 2 hours. The numbers in brackets indicate the number in the party.

The shading on the chart and names shown are bookings that have already been taken.

(a) Copy and complete the table to show which of the following bookings can be accepted.

Hint

  Mr Wong wants a table for four people at half past 11.

  Mrs Yuill wants lunch with three friends at 12 o'clock.

  Mr Wood would like to host a party for eleven people at quarter past one.

  Mr White wants a table for six at 11 a.m.

  Ms Astle wants lunch with a friend at 12 o'clock.

  Mr Richards wants a table for three people at 1 p.m.

(b) What alternative booking could you offer to customers whose bookings you were unable to accept?

4 A chef has found an old recipe for a kipper pie.

The recipe states that this will make four servings.

There are 16 oz in 1 lb, 1 oz = 28.35 g, 1 kg = 2.2 pounds and 1 pint = 0.568 litres

The chef uses past data to decide how much kipper pie to make for this Friday's lunch.

Kipper Pie

8 oz flour

6 oz butter

$\frac{1}{2}$ pint cream

12 oz boned kipper

3 eggs

$\frac{1}{4}$ teaspoon pepper

$\frac{3}{8}$ teaspoon salt

He looks at this data for the number of people who have chosen the fish dish on Fridays in the past month.

Friday	Fish dish	Chicken dish	Beef dish	Vegetarian dish
1	15	23	12	5
2	17	22	16	9
3	22	31	21	6
4	15	28	18	12

(a) The chef knows that there are 60 people booked for lunch this Friday.

Based on this data, decide how many servings of kipper pie the chef should make. Show any calculations you make and how these helped you make your decision.

(b) For the number of servings you chose, write out the ingredients the chef will need using metric measures. Round your answers sensibly.

Hint

47

5 At the end of the evening the waiters put all their tips into the tip box. On Friday evening seven waiters were on duty and the total amount in tips was £83.24.

The table shows how much each of them got in tips.

Name	Winston	Page	Chelsey	Tim	Talia	Tobias	Sophia
Amount of tip	£3.90	£18.00	£4.55	£12.84	£18.90	£16.45	£8.60

The manager, Rob, used to use this rule to share the total tips each evening.

> 'The amount of tip each waiter gets is the total tips divided by the number of waiters.'

(a) How much would each waiter get using this rule?

Some waiters complained that they worked hard to get tips, and therefore they should have a bigger share of the tip box.

Rob decided to change the rule so that each waiter kept half of the tip they received and the other half was put into the tip box. The amount in the tip box was then shared equally by the number of waiters.

(b) Use this rule to work out how much of the £83.24 each of the waiters should get.

6 Mobile Restaurant

Rhys lives in Brighton and runs a small mobile fast-food restaurant.

He drives a trailer round the country selling filled potatoes, side salads and smoothies.
He visits events all over the country.

Sometimes it's cheaper to stay at a hotel rather than drive home and out again the next day.

The running costs for his van and trailer work out at about 35p a kilometre.
A hotel costs about £60 a night.

The distance chart gives the distances of the places he visits.
Rhys estimates that he can average about 40 mph with the trailer attached to his van.

Distances in kilometres

Brighton						
272	Bristol					
95	195	London				
310	233	212	Nottingham			
175	120	95	164	Oxford		
375	295	272	72	225	Sheffield	
105	125	130	272	108	320	Southampton

Rhys has this in his diary

| To change from .... to .... Multiply by .... |
Kilometres	Miles	0.62
Metres	Feet	3.28
Centimetres	Inches	0.39
Litres	Gallons	0.22

For health and safety reasons the counter and food preparation area must be made of single sheets of special plastic (no joins, otherwise bacteria can breed there).

The antibacterial plastic sheet comes in two sizes, 8 feet by 4 feet and 10 feet by 4 feet.

THE HEALTHY SPUD BILL OF FAYRE a baked potato AND

Any two of these (8) fillings

Sour cream and chives	Corned beef and horseradish
3 bean chilli	Broccoli & cheese
Prawn mayonnaise	Chilli con carne
Sautéed mushrooms	Mackerel with fromage frais

Any one of these (12) side salads

Vegetable salad with buttermilk dressing	Cranberry almond green salad
Pecan mandarin orange green salad	Herbed spinach salad
Caesar salad	Sweet and sour spinach salad
Marinated green bean salad	Couscous vegetable salad
Kipper coleslaw	Strawberry asparagus salad
Strawberry melon salad	Chutney rice and fruit salad

(a) According to Rhys, about how long will it take him to drive from his home in Brighton to Southampton?

(b) One weekend Rhys has to do a festival in Sheffield followed by a fair in Nottingham the next day.
How much money could he save by staying overnight in a hotel in Sheffield?

(c) During the summer Rhys has three pop festivals to go to on three consecutive days – beginning in Oxford, followed by Southampton and ending in London.
Rhys doesn't like driving too much.
Plan a route for him to take over the three days to cut his driving time to a minimum. He is willing to pay to stay at hotels to save on driving.

(d) The local authority Health and Safety Department inspects Rhys's food trailer.
There are no problems, but they suggest he re-covers the serving counter with some special plastic.

The counter measures 2 m by 80 cm.

He also needs to replace the food preparation surface and back board. These measure 2 m by 1.2 m and 2 m by 40 cm respectively.

Show how the special plastic sheets can be cut so as to minimise waste.

(e) A customer tells Rhys that there doesn't seem to be much choice on the menu.

Who is correct, the customer or Rhys?

Explain, by reasoning and calculation how you arrived at your answer.

(f) Rhys goes to about 30 events a year.
His van is reasonably economical; it can do about 20 miles to the gallon.
Make a rough estimate, showing all your assumptions, of how much fuel Rhys uses in a year.

Work and Budgets

1

The table shows some information about workers in an office.

Age range	20–29	30–39	40–49	50–59
Male	9	5	4	2
Female	8	12	6	4

(a) The manager has been asked to show this information in a chart.

  (i) Draw a dual bar chart to represent this information.

     Make sure your chart has labelled axes and a title.

  (ii) Draw a pie chart to represent the males, and a pie chart to represent the females.

  (iii) Comment on whether the dual bar chart or the two pie charts present the information more clearly.

Hint

(b) A worker is picked at random to receive a prize draw each week.

  What is the probability that the worker picked is:

  (i) male and 20–29   **(ii)** female and 40–49

  (iii) male and 50–59   **(iv)** female and 50–59?

  Work out the probabilities if there was a separate prize for males, and a separate prize for females.

2 A company has a policy of giving each officer worker a minimum of $14\,\text{m}^2$ working space.

(a) An office is needed for 9 office workers.

What is the least total working space needed for these 9 workers?

(b) Another office has a total of $460\,\text{m}^2$ working space. How many office workers is there space for?

3 A call centre is open from 0800 to 2000. Seven people work in the call centre. The diagram below shows the times worked by each person.

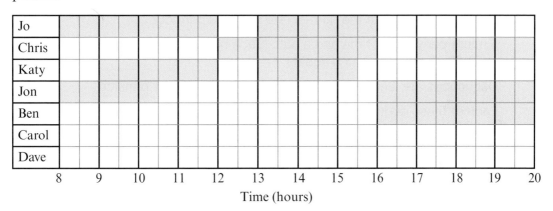

Time (hours)

(a) Work out how many hours each of these people work in the call centre each day.

(b) There needs to be at least three people in the call centre at any one time. List the times when there are fewer than three people in the call centre.

(c) Carol and Dave can each work a shift of 5 hours (plus a break of 1 hour). For both Carol and Dave find:

(i) the starting time

(ii) the finishing time.

You need to make sure you have at least three people in the call centre at any one time.

4 Chris wants to apply for a job as a sales person. He sees three adverts for similar jobs with three different companies, A, B and C.

Work out the annual salary for each job advertised. Take the average sales for these jobs to be £80 000 per year.

A

> ## Sales officer
>
> **£30K per annum**

B

> ## SALES PERSON
>
> **Salary:**
> **£2580 per month**

C

> ## Sales
>
> 5% sales commission plus
> £25,200 annual salary

5 Shazia is comparing two job offers she has been given.

Company A has offered her a job with the following terms:

> 32 hours per week at the normal rate of £8.60 per hour.
>
> 5 hours per week at time and a half. (Each hour is paid at £8.60 plus half as much again.)
>
> Deductions are: 20% for tax, 9% for insurance, 5% for pension
>
> Each of these deductions is made from the original total amount.
>
> You will be paid for 45 weeks of the year.

Hint

Company B has offered her a job with the following terms:

> A salary of £15 560.
>
> 26 days annual leave plus 8 public holidays.
>
> Deductions: 22% tax, 8% for insurance, 4% for pension.

Shazia likes the sound of both of the jobs equally so she decides to choose the one that will give her the most money.

Which company should Shazia work for?

Show your workings and how you reached your answer.

6 Budgeting

Make sure you write down all of your working and answers clearly.

Rhys lives in Meols on the Wirral and is about to start his first job.

The job is at a call centre in Chester. He is paid £7 an hour (including lunch hour).

There are three shifts he could do:
08 00 till 16 00
10 00 till 18 00
12 00 till 20 00

He will get the train to work, changing at Hamilton Square for the Chester train.

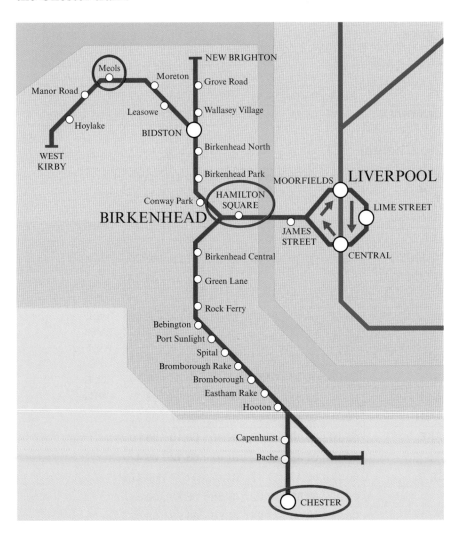

West Kirby to Liverpool Central

WEST KIRBY		05 51		06 21		06 51		07 06	
HOYLAKE		05 54		06 24		06 54		07 09	
MANOR ROAD		05 56		06 26		06 56		07 11	
MEOLS		05 58		06 28		06 58		07 13	
MORETON		06 01		06 31		07 01		07 16	
LEASOWE		06 03		06 33		07 03		07 18	AND
BIDSTON		06 06		06 36		07 06		07 21	AT
NEW BRIGHTON	05 53	-	06 23	-	06 53	-	07 08	-	THESE
GROVE ROAD	05 57	-	06 27	-	06 57	-	07 12	-	TIMES
WALLASEY VILLAGE	05 59	-	06 29	-	06 59	-	07 14	-	PAST THE
BIRKENHEAD NORTH	06 04	06 09	06 34	06 39	07 04	07 09	07 19	07 24	HOUR
BIRKENHEAD PARK	06 06	06 11	06 36	06 41	07 06	07 11	07 21	07 26	UNTIL
CONWAY PARK	06 09	06 14	06 39	06 44	07 09	07 14	07 24	07 29	18 51
HAMILTON SQUARE	06 11	06 16	06 41	06 46	07 11	07 16	07 26	07 31	
JAMES STREET	06 14	06 19	06 44	06 49	07 14	07 19	07 29	07 34	
MOORFIELDS	06 16	06 21	06 46	06 51	07 16	07 21	07 31	07 36	
LIME STREET	06 18	06 23	06 48	06 53	07 18	07 23	07 33	07 38	
LIVERPOOL CENTRAL	06 20	06 25	06 50	06 55	07 20	07 25	07 35	07 40	

Moorfields to Chester

MOORFIELDS	05 41	06 11	06 41	07 11	07 41	08 11	
LIME STREET	05 43	06 13	06 43	07 13	07 43	08 13	
LIVERPOOL CENTRAL	05 45	06 15	06 45	07 15	07 45	08 15	
JAMES STREET	05 47	06 17	06 47	07 17	07 47	08 17	
HAMILTON SQUARE	05 50	06 20	06 50	07 20	07 50	08 20	
BIRKENHEAD CENTRAL	05 52	06 22	06 52	07 22	07 52	08 22	AND
GREEN LANE	05 54	06 24	06 54	07 24	07 54	08 24	AT
ROCK FERRY	05 57	06 27	06 57	07 27	07 57	08 27	THESE
BEBINGTON	05 59	06 29	06 59	07 29	07 59	08 29	TIMES
PORT SUNLIGHT	06 01	06 31	07 01	07 31	08 01	08 31	PAST THE
SPITAL	06 03	06 33	07 03	07 33	08 03	08 33	HOUR
BROMBOROUGH RAKE	06 05	06 35	07 05	07 35	08 05	08 35	UNTIL
BROMBOROUGH	06 07	06 37	07 07	07 37	08 07	08 37	19 11
EASTHAM RAKE	06 10	06 40	07 10	07 40	08 10	08 40	
HOOTON	06 12	06 42	07 12	07 42	08 12	08 42	
CAPENHURST	06 17	06 47	07 17	07 47	08 17	08 47	
BACHE	06 22	06 52	07 22	07 52	08 22	08 52	
CHESTER	06 26	06 56	07 26	07 56	08 26	08 56	

Rhys checks at Meols station for the price of tickets to Chester.
He jots down the information.

Anytime single to Chester £4.05
Anytime return £5.50
Anytime weekly ticket £20

Cheap day return (only starting out after 9:30 am) £4.40

Young person's railcard £24 a year
gives one third off all fares but only after 10 am

(a) Which trains should he catch from Meols to get to work on
time for each of the three shifts? The call centre is about
5 minutes walk from the station.

Each week Rhys works two early shifts (08 00 till 16 00) and a
middle shift (10 00 till 18 00) and a late shift (12 00 till 20 00).

(b) Advise Rhys how he can pay the least to travel to and from
work in a year. In one year Rhys works for 47 weeks.

Use this information to calculate an average weekly figure
for Rhys's travel costs.

Rhys is talking to his friends Maria and Tom about how much money he'll be earning.

> It might seem a lot of money, £7 an hour, but remember 30% is taken for income tax and National Insurance.

> Then there is the cost of travelling to work, and my lunch costs £3 each day.

> Over the last couple of months I spent about £100 on clothes.

> I pay my mother £30 a week for rent.

> There is not much left over for holidays, savings and weekend spending money.

> I save money where I can, so I take a packed lunch. Last month I spent £75 on clothes. I'll try not to buy any more for a couple of months.

> My mother charges me £40 each week but she makes my packed lunch every day.

(c) Draw up a realistic weekly budget for Rhys.

Make sensible estimates for how much he might spend on lunch, clothes and rent. Explain why you made these estimates.

How much does he have left over for holidays, savings and weekend spending money?

The Beauty Therapist

1 This pie chart shows the household expenditure on beauty products in one year in Britain.

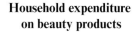

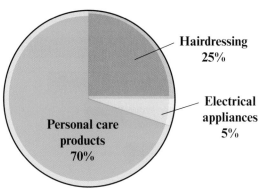

(a) If £20 191 million was spent on beauty products, work out how much was spent on:

   (i) Personal care products.

   (ii) Hairdressing.

   (iii) Electrical appliances.

   Write your answers in figures.

(b) In 2006, £5158 million was spent on hairdressing. This was 24% of the total spent.

Hint

72% of the total was spent on personal care products.

How much was spent on personal care products?

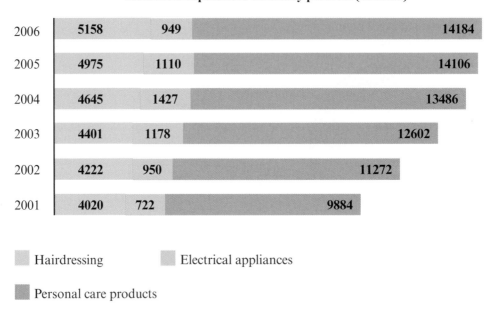

Household expenditure on beauty products (£million)

	Hairdressing	Electrical appliances	Personal care products
2006	5158	949	14184
2005	4975	1110	14106
2004	4645	1427	13486
2003	4401	1178	12602
2002	4222	950	11272
2001	4020	722	9884

(c) **(i)** How much was spent on beauty products in 2002?

(ii) Which area of expenditure has shown the smallest percentage increase over the years 2001 to 2006?

Hint

In 2006, the average expenditure on beauty products was £332.80 per household.

(iii) Work out approximately how many households were included in the statistics for that year.

Give your answer to the nearest million.

(d) Estimate the amount spent on hairdressing in 2007, to the nearest £100 million.

2 Julie and her friends are having a 'Pamper Party'. She has arranged for a beauty therapist to attend from 6.30 p.m. until 9.30 p.m.

The following treatments are available.

Make-up lesson	55 min	£30
Eyebrow shape	15 min	£7
Eyelash tint	10 min	£11
Eyelash extensions	10 min	£5
Bikini wax	15 min	£8
Leg wax	30 min	£14
Manicure	45 min	£15
Ear piercing	10 min	£12.50

The friends give the therapist the following list of treatments they would like.

Clients	Requested treatment		
Julie	Make-up lesson	Leg wax	Ear piercing
Claire	Eyebrow shape	Eyelash tint	Manicure
Jo	Ear piercing	Manicure	Bikini wax
Narinder	Leg wax	Eyebrow shape	Eyelash extensions

The therapist plans her evening's work to ensure each of the friends receives at least one of the treatments she has requested.

Plan her schedule for the evening to maximise her takings.

Hint

3   A beauty salon employs a team of therapists who can offer treatments at the times listed below.
The therapists take a one-hour lunch break.

Beautician	Nails	Hair	Waxing	Facials	Days	Hours
Alana	✗	✓	✗	✓	Mon–Thurs	0800–1500
Sharon	✓	✗	✓	✓	Mon–Fri	0900–1700
Laura	✗	✓	✓	✓	Tues–Fri	0900–1230
Emily	✗	✗	✓	✓	Thurs–Sat	0800–1630
Kelly	✓	✓	✗	✗	Wed–Sat	0900–1630

The therapists earn a basic wage of £7.73 per hour for one speciality. Each additional therapy they can offer increases their hourly rate by 45p.

(a) Work out the weekly wage for each therapist.

(b) Which therapist earns the most money on a Wednesday?

Hint

The salon records the client bookings in a diary with one page for each day. They allow a minimum of one hour per treatment to ensure the clients are not rushed.

Monday					
Therapist	Alana	Sharon	Laura	Emily	Kelly
08 00					
08 30					

The following clients have rung the salon requesting appointments on Thursday. The hours needed for each appointment are shown in the table.

	Nails	Hair	Waxing	Facial	Times
Miss Green	1	2			1 p.m. or 2 p.m.
Mrs Newman		2			3 p.m.
Miss Bright	1	1		1	Early morning
Mrs Wright		2	1		Must leave by 11 a.m.
Miss Pugh		1		1	Must leave by 2.30 p.m.
Mrs Ahmed	1		1	1	Morning
Mrs Lee	1	1	1		Before 10 a.m. or after 2 p.m.
Miss Bakir	1		1	1	Afternoon
Mrs Tanner			1	1	Afternoon
Miss Petran	1			1	Morning
Miss Smith	1	1	1		Lunchtime
Mrs Brady	1		1	1	After 2 p.m.
Miss Williams	1	1		1	Early afternoon

(c) Schedule the appointments for Thursday.

Hint

(d) (i) Which appointment requests could not be booked?

(ii) The salon is going to employ another therapist. Which treatment(s) should they be looking for?

4 Katie-Jo is setting up a beauty salon.
Her set-up costs are shown in the table.

Item	Cost		Quantity
Heater	£59		
Pot of wax	£4.95		15 customers
Spatulas	99p	100	1 per customer
Fabric strips	£2	100	4 per leg
Before-waxing cream	£3.80		
After-waxing cream	£4.25		

She charges £21 for a full leg wax.

(a) How many clients must she treat before she recovers her set-up costs?

(b) How much profit will she make after treating 20 customers?

Hint

Ear piercing   £12.50
(includes cleaning solution and two studs)

In order to provide ear piercing, she goes on a training course at a cost of £75.60 and is provided with the basic kit including the gun with 24 pairs of studs. However, only three bottles of cleaning solution are included in the kit.

A pack of 20 bottles of cleaning solution costs £8.66.

A pack of 12 studs costs £4.83.

(c) How many ear piercings must she complete before she recovers her start-up costs?

5 In order to attract new customers Antonio is offering clients a
mini facial at cost price + 2% to cover fixed costs.

Hint

The facial products needed are listed below.
How much should Antonio charge?
Round your final answer to a sensible selling price.

Product	Cost
Toner 250 ml bottle (10 ml per facial)	£25.00 per bottle
Moisturiser 200 ml bottle (10 ml per facial)	£25.00 per bottle
Cleanser 150 ml bottle (15 ml per facial)	£10.00 per bottle
Face pack (1 per facial)	£1.50 per pack
Exfoliator 500 ml jar (50 ml per facial)	£23.00 per jar
Consumables (towels and cotton wool pads)	£1.23 per customer
Eye tonic 100 ml tube (5 ml per facial)	£43.00 per tube
Tea tree oil 250 ml bottle (5 ml per facial)	£20 per bottle

6 Closing down

Make sure you write down all of your working and answers clearly.

As the Finance Director of Beau Tee, a chain of hair and beauty salons, you have to decide which salon or salons to close down due to a recession and a reduction in disposable income.
You have to be sure that the salons you retain are profitable and will ensure the ongoing success of the chain.

Tables 1–3 give this year's details for each of the salons and include staff details, turnover and percentage profit, and other information.

Table 1 Staff details, including number of staff, mean average staff cost

Salon name	Number of equivalent full-time staff	Mean average monthly staff cost (per member of staff)
Beau Tee Lilyport	3	£1457
Beau Tee Abergele*	9	£1373
Beau Tee Liverpool	7	£1643
Beau Tee Breeze Town**	6	£1273
Beau Tee Thirsk**	8	£1204
Beau Tee Bullington	10	£1216
Beau Tee Whitehall*	9	£2000

Table 2 Sales and percentage profit this year

Salon name	Turnover (total sales)	Percentage of sales that is profit
Beau Tee Lilyport	£132 888	18
Beau Tee Abergele*	£340 231	8
Beau Tee Liverpool	£245 888	27
Beau Tee Breeze Town**	£231 433	13
Beau Tee Thirsk**	£235 760	14
Beau Tee Bullington	£330 067	−5
Beau Tee Whitehall*	£190 877	13

Table 3 Other information, including years trading and competitors

Salon name	Years trading	Competitors in area
Beau Tee Lilyport	8	2
Beau Tee Abergele*	5	3
Beau Tee Liverpool	3	4
Beau Tee Breeze Town**	2	1
Beau Tee Thirsk**	23	2
Beau Tee Bullington	6 months	0
Beau Tee Whitehall*	6	9

Next year's profits:
Beau Tee Liverpool is projected to make a £50 000 loss.
Stores marked * are projected to make the same profit as in the previous year.
Stores marked ** are projected to make £20 000 more profit than in the previous year.
All other stores are projected to make £50 000 more profit than in the previous year.

(a) Construct Table 4 showing:

    (i) Profits this year   (ii) Projected profits next year

(b) Consider the information in Tables 1–4 and recommend which stores should continue to trade.
Justify your recommendations with figures.

Business

1 Daniel is a sales representative working for Games & Toys Ltd.

He has to plan his work schedule for the year.

During 2010, Daniel has 30 days of holiday plus the following bank holidays: Jan 1st, April 2nd, April 5th, May 3rd, May 30th, Aug 30th, Dec 27th and Dec 28th.

He must always spend some days each month in his office.
His office days are shown in the table.
The remaining working days are spent visiting customers.

Months	Weekdays	Holidays	Working days	Office days	Customer days
January	22	4	18	5	13
February	20	0	20	7	13
March	22			7	
April	22			7	
May	21			6	
June	22			7	
July	23			7	
August	21			7	
September	22			7	
October	22			6	
November	21			7	
December	23			7	
Totals	261	38		80	

(a) (i) Copy and complete the table to show a possible plan of Daniel's working year for 2010. The first two months are done for you.

Note: Daniel must use all his 38 days of holiday (30 + 8 days of bank holidays) during this year.

Hint

(ii) What percentage of the 18 working days in January did Daniel spend visiting customers?
Give your answer correct to 1 decimal place.

(iii) What percentage of the total number of working days did Daniel spend visiting customers?
Give your answer correct to 1 decimal place.

The following table shows Daniel's target and actual sales for each month in 2010.

Month	Target sales in £	Actual sales in £	Bonus sales	Bonus in £
January	10 000	8565	–	0
February	20 000	14 680	–	0
March	25 000	30 254	5254	131.35
April	20 000	24 806	4806	120.15
May	20 000	29 808		
June	25 000	36 552		
July	20 000	17 726		
August	20 000	14 280		
September	30 000	43 208		
October	40 000	69 545		
November	40 000	60 424		
December	40 000	39 506		
Totals	£310 000			

(b) **(i)** Work out Daniel's total sales for 2010.

(ii) Each month, Daniel works out how much he has made above his target sales figure. This is called his bonus sales. He calculates 2.5% of his bonus sales to find his bonus.

Copy and complete the table to show the bonus earned each month. January to April are done for you.

(iii) Daniel earns a basic wage of £1200 each month. At the end of each year, he is paid an additional bonus of 1% of all sales above target.
Work out Daniel's total earnings for 2010.

Hint

2 The Town Council advertised for a Finance Assistant and placed the following advertisement in the local newspaper:

THE DAILY JOURNAL

Positions vacant

Finance Assistant wanted

We are looking for an individual with a keen interest in working in a financial administration team.

You will need to demonstrate knowledge and experience of invoice payment procedures and have good IT and communication skills. Benefits include a generous annual leave allowance and the opportunity to join the Local Government Pension Scheme. Application forms on request. Tel 01234567

(a) The cost of placing this advertisement was £70 for the first 4 lines, after the job title, plus £12 for each extra line.
Work out the total cost of placing this advertisement in the local newspaper.

(b) Nine people applied for the job.

Four of the nine applicants are chosen for interviews.
The table below is used to make this decision.

The table shows a grade rating for each of the categories of *Qualifications*, *Experience* and *Letter of Application*.

Name	Qualifications rating	Experience rating	Letter rating	Total rating
Zubair Ahmed	B	C	B	
Stephen McKiernan	A	B	B	
David Pearson	C	B	A	
Fozia Patel	A	B	A	
Jeremy Lander	A	D	C	
Emma Steele	B	A	C	
Michelle Kearns	A+	B	A	
Gail Porter	C	B	D	
Carlton Teale	B	A+	C	

Which four applicants should be chosen for interview?
Explain how you reached your decision.

Hint

(c) The four applicants are invited for interviews at 09 30.

The Chief Executive wants to speak to them all together for 30 minutes and then take them all on a tour of the departments.

They are then each to have an informal 15-minute interview with the Chief Finance Officer and an informal 15-minute interview with the Housing Director.

The four candidates are to have lunch together with the Chief Finance Officer. Lunch will last for one hour.

After lunch each candidate is to have a formal 30-minute interview with a panel. The panel consists of the Chief Executive, the Chief Finance Officer, the Housing Director and the Head of Personnel.

(i) Work out a schedule for all of the interviews, the tour and lunch so that everything is completed by 15 00.

Hint

(ii) Work out a timetable for when the Chief Executive, the Chief Finance Officer, the Housing Director and the Head of Personnel are each needed for the interview process.

3 Joe Lake is setting up a business selling small toys, that he imports from China, for childrens' party bags and christmas stocking fillers.

(a) As part of his market research he asked 500 people how much they were prepared to pay for a toy.

The results are shown in the bar chart.

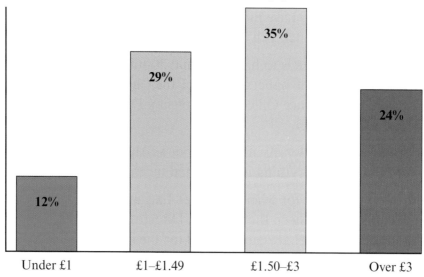

How much will customers pay?

- 12% — Under £1
- 29% — £1–£1.49
- 35% — £1.50–£3
- 24% — Over £3

(i) How many people were prepared to pay over £1.49?

(ii) Show the survey results on an accurate pie chart.

(b) Joe wants to work out an estimate of the amount of money he will need to spend in starting and running the business for six months.

He uses the following formula:

> Costs = initial expenses
> + (monthly costs × number of months)

His monthly costs and a range of estimates for the initial expenses are as follows.

Initial expenses		Monthly costs	
Legal fees	£200–£ 400	Wages	£1300
Office supplies	£ 100–£ 300	Rent	£ 400
Office equipment	£600–£1000	Others	£ 300
Design	£ 40–£ 60	Total	£2000
Brochure	£ 100–£ 300		
Website	£200–£ 400		
Total	?		

(i) Make an estimate of the total initial expenses based on Joe's estimates.

Show how you got your estimate and state any reasons you chose this way.

(ii) Use the formula to estimate Joe's costs for the first six months.

(c) **(i)** Estimate the amount of money he needs to make each month to have not lost any money after six months?

[Hint]

(ii) Joe imports the toys at a cost of 97p each.
In the first month, he decides to sell them at a price of £3.00 for each toy.
How many toys does he need to sell to cover his monthly costs?

(iii) Based on his survey results, if he offers the toys to 2000 customers, predict how how many toys he will sell at the price of £3.00?

(iv) If he sells the number of toys you predicted, how much profit or loss will he make in the first month?
Show how you got your answer.

(v) If Joe decreased the price to £1.49 in the second month, what profit or loss would he make if he offered the toys to 5000 people? Assume that all of his costs are the same for each month.

(d) The table shows the **actual** numbers of toys Joe sold in the first six months of business.

Month	1	2	3	4	5	6
Sales	1248	2462	3486	3564	4540	4622

(i) Work out the mean, median and range of the number of toys sold per month.

(ii) Joe sold the toys for £2.49 for each of the first six months. Was his business running at a profit or at a loss, and how much profit or loss was made?

(iii) The numbers of toys sold in the next six months of business are shown in the table below.

Month	7	8	9	10	11	12
Sales	3532	4876	5954	3358	2542	3509

By considering the mean, median and range, compare the sales of toys in the first six months with those of the next six months.

(iv) Give a possible reason why the sales of toys were so high during the ninth month.

(v) Could Joe reach any conclusions about the trend in sales by using the comparisons made in part **(iii)** of the two six-month periods? Explain why or why not.

4   Ramla's Greeting Cards

Ramla always wanted to work for herself.

She is quite artistic with a good sense of colour, so thought of making greetings cards.

She could sell them at the local market.

The market is open three days a week, giving her time to make the cards as well as sell them.

Before she begins, Ramla jots down a list of costs and expenses.

Cost of card for each card: about 2p
Cost of ink for printer: about 6p per card
Cost of glitter, stickers etc.: about 5p per card

The costs below are all called fixed expenses; Ramla needs to pay them however many cards she sells.

Rent of market stall: £40 a day
Costs of heating etc. at home
whilst making cards: £50 a week
Wages: I'll pay myself about
£200 a week
Insurance: £10 a week

I'll also need to buy these which
I will pay for over 10 weeks.
Software to print the cards: £40
A good quality printer: £120
A second-hand computer: £240

Before she starts in business Ramla asks some friends what is the most they would pay for a greetings card.

Here are the results of her survey.

The most I would pay for a greetings card is:	Tally
£1.00	卌
£1.50	卌 卌 卌
£2.00	卌 卌 卌
£2.50	卌 卌 卌 ||
£3.00	|||
£3.50		

Ramla looks at her survey results and decides to investigate what would happen if she charged £1.50 per card. She sets up a spreadsheet to investigate the effects of altering her selling price.

Ramla Braithwaite Card Stall Prices

	A	B	C	D	E
1	Selling Price	Materials	Cards sold in 10 weeks		
2	£ 1.50	£ 0.13	600		
3					
4	Expenses each week				
5	Stall rent	£ 120.00			
6	Home heating etc.	£ 50.00			
7	Wages	£ 200.00			
8	Insurance	£ 10.00			
9					
10	Computer purchases				
11	to be paid back				
12	over 10 weeks	£ 400.00			
13					
14	Total money collected				
15	in 10 weeks	£ 900.00			
16					
17	Total paid out				
18	in 10 weeks	£ 2,778.00	Overall profit in 10 weeks		£ 1,878.00

(a) Ramla is really pleased with the profit.
In fact it seems too good to be true!
Check the following three formulae she used.

Correct those that are wrong by either writing out the formula in words or writing the correct formula Ramla should have entered into the spreadsheet.

(i) To calculate the amount that appears in cell B15 she used this formula.

Money collected in 10 weeks = number of cards sold × price per card

The formula she typed into the spreadsheet in cell B15 is:

| B15 | ▼ | fx | =A2*C2 |

(ii) To calculate the amount that appears in cell B18 she used this formula.

Money paid out in 10 weeks = 10 × (stall rent + home heating + insurance)
+ total money collected
+ number of cards sold × materials cost

The formula she typed into the spreadsheet in cell B18 is:

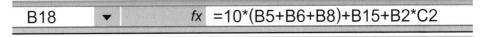

| B18 | ▼ | fx | =10*(B5+B6+B8)+B15+B2*C2 |

(iii) To calculate the amount that appears in cell E18 she used this formula.

Overall profit in 10 weeks = money paid out in 10 weeks
− money collected in 10 weeks

The formula she typed into the spreadsheet in cell E18 is:

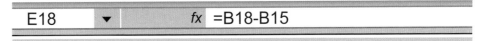

| E18 | ▼ | fx | =B18-B15 |

(b) How many cards will she need to sell over ten weeks in order to break even? (This means zero profit – but Ramla still has her wages!)

(c) Can Ramla realistically ever make a profit from her business? Remember that you'll need to convince her either to carry on or to quit, so it's important to get your facts (and numbers) right!   Hint

(d) How might Ramla have improved her survey at the beginning?

Summer Holiday

Mark and Rehana and their daughters Mia and Zara go to Zante, one of the Greek islands, for their summer holiday.

Mia is 12 years old and Zara is 7 years old.

1 The table below shows the cost, in pounds (£), for each adult staying at the Beach Hotel in Zante. The cost for each child is shown in the bottom two rows.

Nights	7	10	11	14
01 May–13 May	279	295	299	305
14 May–25 May	415	425	429	445
26 May–10 Jun	375	405	439	475
11 Jun–24 Jun	405	445	499	509
25 Jun–08 Jul	435	475	485	529
09 Jul–15 Jul	455	495	509	565
16 Jul–22 Jul	475	549	569	625
23 Jul–17 Aug	505	575	595	669
18 Aug–24 Aug	479	529	539	595
25 Aug–31 Aug	435	479	489	529
01 Sep–15 Sep	419	445	455	495
1st child	139	149	149	149
2nd child	FREE	FREE	FREE	FREE

(a) Work out the range of the costs for 7 nights for one adult.

(b) Between which two dates is the cost the least expensive for 14 nights?

(c) What is the cost for one adult staying at the Beach Hotel for 7 nights from the 12th June?

(d) Give one reason why the costs are at their highest in July and August.

Mark, Rehana, Mia and Zara decide to stay at the Beach Hotel for 14 nights from the 2nd August.

August

M	Tu	W	Th	F	Sa	Su
					1	2
3	4	5	6	7	8	9
10	11	12	13	14	15	16
17	18	19	20	21	22	23
24	25	26	27	28	29	30
31						

(e) **(i)** What is the cost for one adult?

(ii) Work out the cost for the whole family.
Is it below their £1200 budget? Show your reasoning.

(f) Mia and Zara go back to school on the 3rd September.

Give alternative dates when the family could stay in this hotel for 14 nights for under the £1200 budget.

(g) The Beach Hotel is going to close for the winter on the last Sunday in September. What date will it close for winter?

2 The table below shows some flight details from London to Zante.

Flight	Nights	Day/time of departure	Day/time of return	Dates	Supplement (per person)
18106	7/14	Fri 06 50	Fri 14 40	1 May–23 Oct	£25
18106	11	Fri 06 50	Tues 15 00	1 May–16 Oct	£0
18106	10	Fri 06 50	Mon 22 25	1 May–11 Sep	£25
18107	7/14	Sun 14 55	Sun 22 35	3 May–20 Sep	£35
18108	7/14	Sun 06 05	Sun 13 55	3 May–25 Oct	£45
18109	7/14	Mon 14 35	Mon 22 25	4 May–14 Sep	£25
18109	11	Mon 14 35	Fri 14 40	4 May–21 Sep	£0
18110	7/14	Tues 23 55	Wed 07 30	30 Jun–8 Sep	£0
18111	7/14	Tues 07 00	Tues 15 00	5 May–20 Oct	£25
18111	10	Tues 07 00	Fri 14 40	5 May–20 Oct	£0

(a) If they leave on the 2nd August, which two flights could Mark and his family take?
(The calendar for August is given in question **1**.)

(b) Which flight do you think they should take.
Give a reason for your answer.

(c) The flight takes $3\frac{1}{4}$ hours.
The time in Zante is two hours ahead of UK time.
What is the local time of arrival in Zante of flight 18107?

> Hint

(d) The time of the return flight from Zante to London is 22 35 local time in Zante. What is the expected time of arrival in London, UK time, if the flight again takes $3\frac{1}{4}$ hours?

3 The diagram shows the only remaining seats available on flight 18107.

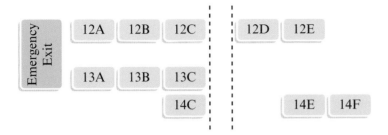

(a) A seat is selected at random.

What is the probability that this seat will be on row 13?

(b) The passengers still to be seated are:

Mark, Rehana, Mia and Zara,

Mr and Mrs Johnson and their son Peter,

Adnan and his partner Rea,

David Smith and Briony Dee who are each travelling alone.

Allocate a sensible seat number for each of these passengers.

| Hint |

(c) Three other passengers, Angela, Michelle and Daniel, occupy seats in row 11. Show all the different ways in which these passengers can be seated. One has already been done for you.

11A	11B	11C
Angela	Michelle	Daniel

4 Each passenger is allowed to take one item of hand luggage onto the aeroplane. The maximum allowable dimensions are 56 cm × 32 cm × 24 cm, as shown in the diagram of a cuboid below.

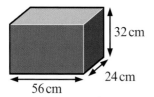

(a) The dimensions of Rehana's bag are:

20 inches × 12 inches × 9 inches

Will she be allowed to take this bag onto the aeroplane? (1 inch = 2.54 cm)

You must show all working to justify your answer.

(b) Mia has a choice between two bags – their dimensions are shown below.

Which of these bags should she choose to take onto the aeroplane?

Give reasons for your answers.

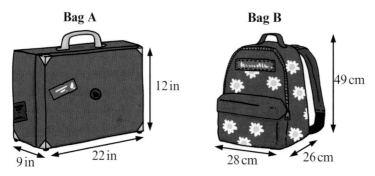

Bag A

Bag B

(c) On Zara's flight each passenger is allowed to carry up to 100 ml of liquid in their hand luggage. Zara has a 0.33 litre can of cola. Can she take it on the plane?

5 At the bank, Mark changed £500 into euros (€).

The exchange rate was £1 = €1.24.

(a) How many euros should Mark get?

(b) The bank charged commission of 1.5% on £500.
How much did the bank take in commission?

(c) Mark was given a ready reckoner to convert between euros (€) and pounds (£).

Copy and complete this ready reckoner.

Pounds (£)	Euros (€)
1	1.24
2	2.48
...	3.72
4	4.96
5	6.20
10	...
20	24.80
50	...
...	124.00
200	...

Hint

(d) Mia wanted to buy a new pair of sunglasses. In London, a pair of sunglasses cost £28. In Zante the identical pair of sunglasses cost €31. Mia bought the cheaper pair of sunglasses.

  (i) Where did Mia buy her sunglasses?

  (ii) How much did she save by buying the cheaper pair?
Give your answer in pounds (£). (Use the table to help.)

(e) The same pair of sunglasses in the USA cost $40.
If the exchange rate was £1 = $1.92, are the sunglasses more or less expensive than the pair Mia bought?

(f) Mark and his family went out for a meal in Zante. The cost of the meal was €92.45. Mark decided to give a tip of 10%.

What did the meal cost altogether?

Give your answer to the nearest euro.

(g) A large ice cream costs €2.60. A small ice cream costs €1.80.
Zara buys four ice creams. She only has a €10 note.

What are the possible sizes of ice creams that Zara buys for her family?

(h) On his return to London, Mark changed €145 back into pounds (£). The exchange rate for this was £1 = €1.28.

How much should Mark have in GBP? (GBP stands for British pounds.)

6 The diagrams show the average daily maximum temperature and the average daily hours of sunshine in Zante and in London from April to October.

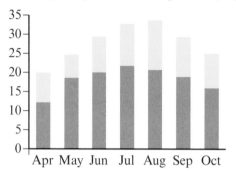

Average daily maximum temperature (°C)

Zante

London

Average daily hours of sunshine

	Apr	May	Jun	Jul	Aug	Sep	Oct
	7	9	11	13	12	9	6
	5	6	7	6	6	5	3

(a) Estimate the July average daily maximum temperature in:

    (i) London.   **(ii)** Zante.

(b) In which of the months shown is the difference between the average daily maximum temperatures:

    (i) greatest?   **(ii)** least?

(c) Of the months shown, which months in London are colder than any in Zante?

(d) Work out the total number of hours of April sunshine in London.

> Hint

(e) Work out the mean daily number of hours of sunshine in Zante from April to October.

> Hint

    Give your answer correct to 2 decimal places.

(f) Mark doesn't understand temperatures in °C (degrees Celsius) and wants to know the highest and lowest temperatures recorded in Zante in °F (degrees Fahrenheit). Mia helps him using this formula:

$$F = \frac{9 \times C}{5} + 32$$

where F stands for °F and C stands for °C.

    What are the highest and lowest temperatures recorded in Zante in degrees Fahrenheit?

(g) Mark wants to know if the temperature in April in Zante, on average, is warmer than 78 °F. Rewrite the formula to help Mark do this. Is the temperature higher than 78 °F?

7 During their holiday in Zante, Mark wants to hire a car.
The cost is €94 and then €25 per day.

(a) Work out the cost of hiring the car for 6 days.

Hint

(b) Mr Johnson hires a similar car. He pays €319.

Work out the number of days that Mr Johnson hired the car.

(c) The map above shows the island of Zante. Mark drove
the car from Limni Keriou to Volimes passing through
Agios Leon.
Estimate the number of kilometres for this journey.
The scale is given on the map.

Hint

(d) The journey took 1½ hours. Estimate the average speed.

Hint

(e) Mark toured around the island. He drove from Lithakia
to Agios Leon, Alikanas, Drossia, Amboula, Akrotiri,
Zakynthos and then back to Lithakia.
Estimate, in kilometres, the length of the perimeter road
on the island of Zante.
About how long would it take to drive right around the island?

8 Holiday hotel

Make sure you write down all of your working and answers clearly.

You are the owner of a small hotel in Zante. Your hotel has 12 rooms. You seem to have had a good season during the summer holidays.

These tables show your income and expenditure.

Income

Prices per person
(Charges are made according to the week of arrival.)

Nights	23 Jul–17 Aug	18 Aug–24 Aug	25 Aug–31 Aug	01 Sep–15 Sep	1st child	2nd child
7	505	479	435	419	139	FREE
14	669	595	529	495	149	FREE

Room occupancy

Room	10 Aug–17 Aug		18 Aug–24 Aug		25 Aug–31 Aug		01 Sep–08 Sep	
	Adult	Child	Adult	Child	Adult	Child	Adult	Child
1	2	2	2	2	2	1	1	
2	2		2		1	3	2	
3	1	1			1	2	2	
4	2	3	2	2	2		2	
5	3		2	1	2	2	2	2
6	1	1	1	1	1	1	1	1
7	2		2		2		2	
8	1	2	1	2	2	2	2	2
9	2	3			2	2	2	2
10	3		3		2	1		
11	2		2					
12	2		2	1	2	1		
Total								

Expenses

Basic costs
- £7.00 per day to clean an occupied room
- £3.00 per person per day for breakfast
- £4.00 per room per day for laundry of sheets and towels in an occupied room
- £50 per week to clean the pool
- £200 per week to clean the public building

Staff

The average wage for an employee is £9.00 per hour.

The working week is 40 hours.

You employ 9 staff.

(a) Use the room occupancy schedule and the table of prices to show your income.

Hint

(b) Use the basic cost table and the staff rates to show your expenses.

Hint

(c) Do you think that the season has been good?

Justify your answer using the data provided.

Police

1 Here is a plan view of a police car.

Hint

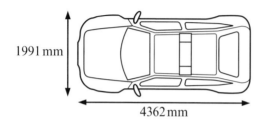

1991 mm

4362 mm

A parking space is needed for this car.
Estimate the area of the parking space. Give your answer in m².

2 The area used for parking at a police station is to be marked out with parking spaces for cars and vans. The vehicles using this area will park side by side in a single row. The width of the parking spaces used for each of the cars and each of the vans will be 2.5 m and 2.9 m respectively. The total of the widths of all the parking spaces must not be greater than 59 m.

It is estimated that the number of vans to the number of cars parking in this area will be between the ratio of 1:1 and 2:1.

Find the number of parking spaces needed for each of these vehicles to make the best use of this area.

3 Here is a diagram of the road network in Weyshore.

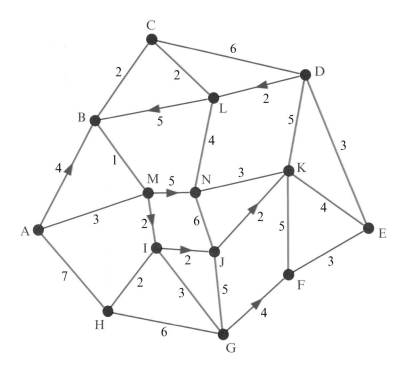

In the diagram, lines represent roads, arrows represent one-way roads, circles represent junctions and numbers give the shortest times, in minutes, to drive between the junctions.

There is an accident at junction A.
Police cars are located at junctions F and J when the alarm is raised.
A controller wants to send one of the police cars to the accident.

(a) Which police car should the controller send?

Hint

(b) A police station is to be built in Weyshore.

Where would you build the police station?
Explain your answer.

4 There are several pieces of technology that police use to help them in their everyday jobs.

- Speed cameras are used to enforce traffic laws.
- Breathalysers are used to check the alcohol levels of drivers.
- CCTV cameras are used to help police town centres.

(a) All speed cameras are set to trigger when any vehicle is travelling at over the relevant speed limit but allow for a 10% error. They are set according to their position.

   (i) Calculate the minimum speed that the camera would be triggered in a 30 mph zone.

   (ii) Compare the speeds needed to trigger the speed camera in a 70 mph zone to that needed in 40 mph zone. What is the difference?

(b) Some cameras do not have film in them and therefore are just present to deter speeding vehicles.

   The probability that there is film in a particular camera is 0.72.

   The probability that a vehicle is speeding is 0.05.

   Work out the probability that the next two cars will both be caught speeding by this camera.

> Hint

(c) A breathalyser shows the amount of alcohol in the blood by checking the breath.

   The legal limit for driving is for 0.08% of the blood to be alcohol. How much alcohol, in millilitres, is allowed if there are approximately 8 pints of blood in the average body?

> Hint

(d) A CCTV camera is attached to a building or lamppost to help prevent crime. In Weyshore, a CCTV camera is mounted on the corner of a building near the Town Hall. The lens is set to view a 60° angle from the centre – this is 30° to the left and 30% to the right. The mounting of the camera allows it to turn through 160°. What is the angle range that the camera can view?

5 The diagram shows the plan and side elevation of a safety cone.

Plan

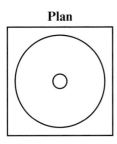

Side elevation

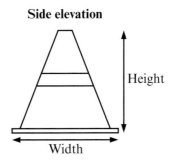

Height

Width

The area of the square base of the safety cone is $0.25\,\text{m}^2$.

The height and the width of the safety cone are in the ratio $4:5$.

(a) Work out the height of this safety cone.
Give your answer in centimetres.

(b) Design your own safety cone. The height and the width of
your safety cone should be in the ratio $7:5$. Draw an accurate
diagram to show the side elevation of your safety cone.

(c) Safety cones should be placed with centres $2\,\text{m}$ apart to
prevent parking along a road. If the road is 1.75 miles, how
many cones are needed to prevent parking anywhere along
the road?

Hint

6 A Chief of Police wants to appoint a constable to each of six departments. The departments are the Marine Unit (MU), the Dog Section (DS), the Criminal Investigation Department (CID), the Operational Support Unit (OSU), the Special Escort Group (SEG) and International Deployment (ID).

There are six suitable applicants. This table shows which departments each applicant is qualified to join.

Candidate	Department
Peter Davis	ID, CID, MU, SEG
Amir Khan	MU, DS, CID
Rosemary Blakely	CID, SEG
Stephanie Fry	OSU, DS
Adam Stockwell	CID, SEG
Harry Palmer	MU, OSU, ID, CID

(a) Write down the names of the applicants who are qualified to join both the Marine Unit and International Deployment.

(b) One of these six applicants is chosen at random. Write down the probability that this applicant is qualified to join the Special Escort Group.

(c) Assuming that these applicants have no preferences about which department they join, show that it is possible for the Chief of Police to appoint a constable to each of the six departments.

7 This table gives information about the numbers and the types of offence committed in Weyshore from 1985 to 2010.

Offence	1985	1990	1995	2000	2005	2010
Violence	567	576	589	596	611	627
Robbery	108	130	120	N	127	131
Burglary	58	54	53	50	44	41
Theft, handling	379	415	456	489	462	420
Fraud, forgery	146	142	148	139	146	145
Criminal damage	187	180	183	318	389	412
Drugs	468	453	430	411	457	463

(N = number not available)

(a) Find an estimate for the value of N in the table.

(b) Explain how the numbers of offences committed in Weyshore have changed from 1985 to 2010.

You should include a variety of graphs to illustrate your findings.

8 Who dunnit?

Make sure you write down all of your working and answers clearly.

A crime has been committed! Miss Bickerton's car has been stolen. The suspect had big feet and above average height for their gender. In the UK, the mean height for males is 176 cm and for females is 164 cm.

Information on the suspects

The bar charts and table summarise the information available.

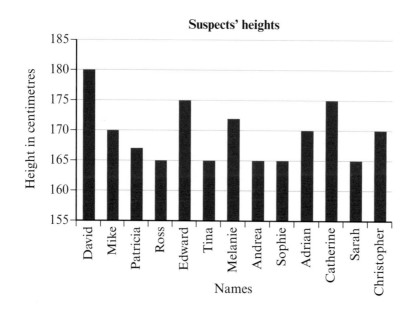

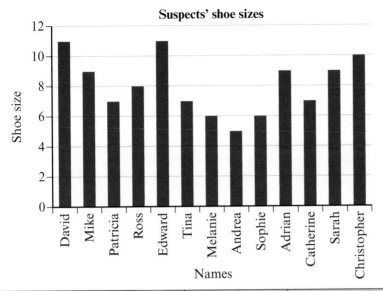

Suspects' shoe sizes

Suspect	Has driving licence	In country at time of crime	Previous convictions for stealing cars
David	✓	✓	2
Mike	✓	✓	3
Patricia		✓	4
Ross	✓	✓	5
Edward		✓	2
Tina	✓	✓	7
Melanie	✓	✓	3
Andrea		✓	7
Sophie	✓		3
Adrian		✓	0
Catherine	✓	✓	0
Sarah		✓	0
Christopher	✓	✓	1

You also know the following probabilities about the crime.

P(female) = 0.4   P(previous convictions) = 0.8

(a) Summarise the information in a table for males and a table for females. Decide whether each suspect has a high, medium or low liklihood of being the criminal.

(b) Suggest who could be the thief. Give reasons for your answer.

Golf

1 John and Don play a game of golf.

Here is the scorecard for their game.

Hole	Length (yards)	Par	Number of shots	
			John	Don
1	371	3	4	3
2	493	4	5	4
3	245	3	4	4
4	438	5	4	7
5	408	4	4	4
6	418	5	5	4
7	362	3	3	3
8	318	3	5	4
9	434	4	4	6
Total	**3487**	**34**		

(a) How many shots did Don take on Hole 2?

(b) Which player took 4 shots on Hole 9?

(c) On which hole did John take the fewest shots?

(d) Find the median length of the holes.

Par on the scorecard refers to the number of shots a good player is expected to take on each hole.

(e) Is there a relationship between the par of a hole and its length? Give a reason for your answer.

John took a total of 38 shots in the game. This is 4 shots over par.

(f) How many shots was Don over par?

A player loses a hole if he takes more shots than the other player.

(g) How many holes did John win?

This table gives information about how to score each hole.

Result	Win	Draw	Lose
Points	1	0.5	0

A player wins a game if he scores more points than the other player.

(h) Which player won the game? Give a reason for your answer.

2 John and Don play another round of golf.

John uses his favourite club, a 6-iron, for his first shot on each of the holes from Hole 1 to Hole 8. Here are the lengths, in yards, of these first shots.

148   153   159   169   168   162   161   158

(a) Work out the average length of John's first shots.

There is a ditch on Hole 9. The ditch is 140 m from the start of the hole. John does not want to hit the ball into the ditch.
Don advises John **not** to use a 6-iron on this hole.

(b) Is this good advice? Explain your answer.
        (1 yard = 0.9144 metres)

3

John and Don have played 10 games of golf. John can win (W), lose (L) or draw (D) a game. Here are his results.

Game	1	2	3	4	5	6	7	8	9	10
Result	L	L	D	D	D	D	D	W	W	W

The result for one of these games is picked at random.

(a) Show on a numerical scale from 0 to 1 the probability that this result will be a draw.

John and Don are going to play another game.

(b) John says he has a 3 in 10 chance of winning this game.

   (i) Explain why he may be right.

  (ii) Explain why he may be wrong.

4 John and Don played five games of golf on a short course in the last two weeks. Here are the times taken, in hours and minutes, for them to play the five games.

1 h 58 min, 1 h 29 min, 1 h 29 min, 1 h 42 min, 1 h 37 min

(a) Work out the average time taken to play these five games. Give your answer in hours and minutes.

`Hint`

On another day John and Don decide to play as many games of golf as they can during the day. The golf course opens at 08 00 and closes at 17 00 and they will take a break of at least 20 minutes between each game.

(b) Draw up a possible timetable for the games of golf they will play.

5 Here is a scale diagram of the first four holes at a golf club.

Hint

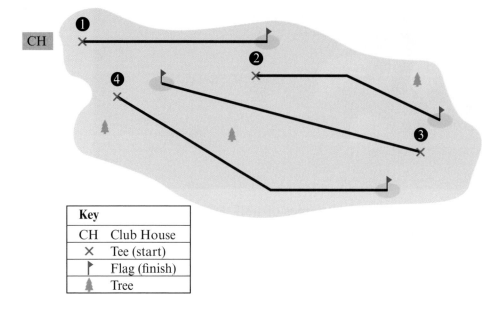

Key	
CH	Club House
✕	Tee (start)
⚑	Flag (finish)
♠	Tree

The length of Hole 1 is 200 m.

It takes a player about five to ten minutes to set up and take the shots needed for each hole.

Estimate how long will it take for three players to complete these first four holes.

6 Golf balls have a diameter of 4 cm. They are sold in boxes of different sizes.

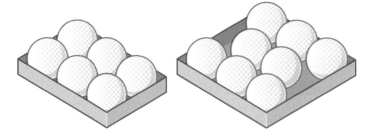

Design boxes for 6, 8, 12, 15 and 20 golf balls.

Draw an accurate net for each box.

7 This table gives information about the members of a golf club.

Players			Non-players
Senior male	**Senior female**	**Junior**	**Social**
320	192	128	128

(a) Work out the ratio of non-playing members to playing members.

(b) Work out the ratio of senior players to junior players.
Give your ratio in its simplest form.

(c) What fraction of the members are junior players?

Give your fraction in its simplest form.

(d) What percentage of the players are senior female players?

This table gives information about the membership fees at the golf club.

Membership fee per person		
Senior	**Junior**	**Social**
£240	£140	£45

(e) Work out the total amount of money collected by the club in membership fees.

The golf club wants to increase the total amount of money collected in membership fees to £160 000.

(f) Assuming that the membership of the club remains the same, suggest new membership fees for the golf club.

The committee decides to keep the membership fees the same and advertise for more members. From previous history they work out they are likely to get about another 80 members in total.

(g) If the ratio of senior to junior players and the ratio of players to non-players stay about the same, is it possible to generate the £160 000 if the fees are kept the same?
Show your working.

8 Crazy golf

Make sure you write down all of your working and answers clearly.

Amy and her brother Tom like playing crazy golf.

They sometimes play on the local council's crazy golf courses.

Prices	Prices per round Wimbledon Park	Prices per round Sir Joseph Hood
Adult	£3.30	£2.00
Junior	£1.75	£1.00
Family (2 adults and 2 children)	£8.00	£5.00

No booking required, just turn up, pay and play. All equipment is supplied.

Their Uncle Richard has a large back garden.

Here is a rough plan of his back garden; unfortunately he still works in feet!

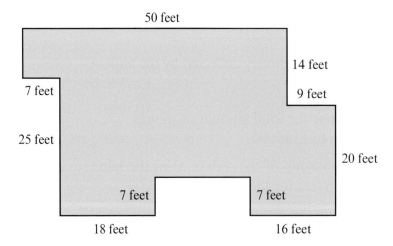

Amy and Tom play as juniors.
They usually play crazy golf at Wimbledon Park.

During the summer they play about three times a week.

(a) **(i)** How much does it cost them to play crazy golf over the summer holidays?

     (ii) How much could they save by playing at Sir Joseph Hood instead?

Amy sees an advert in the free local newspaper for a crazy golf starter set.

They ask Uncle Richard if they could make a small crazy golf course in his back garden. He agrees, providing they show him a scale plan first.

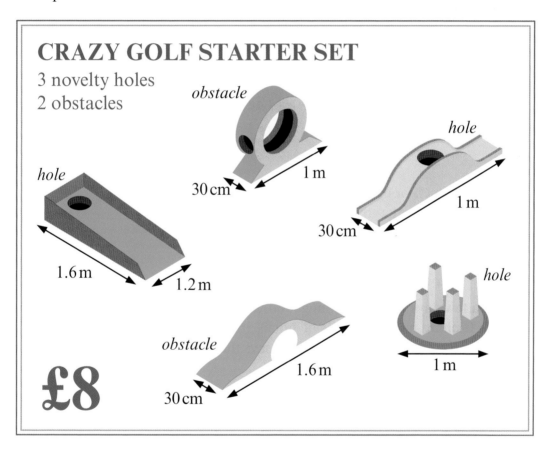

CRAZY GOLF STARTER SET

3 novelty holes
2 obstacles

obstacle

hole

30 cm   1 m

hole

30 cm   1 m

hole

1.6 m   1.2 m

obstacle

30 cm   1.6 m   1 m

£8

(b) Draw a scale plan of a suitable crazy golf course for the garden using just the starter set.
Use a scale of 0.5 cm = 1 foot.
Try to use as much of the garden as possible.

At the local council crazy golf courses, clubs and balls are provided free. Amy and Tom will have to provide their own as well as pay £8 for the starter kit. They look on the internet and jot down some prices.

Golf clubs for crazy golf

| £4 | £15 | £7.50 | £7 |
| £9 | £10.25 | £11.25 | |

Golf balls

3 for £6.99	12 for £14.99	15 for £19.99
6 for £8.50	12 for £34.98	15 for £20
	6 for £7.49	

(c) **(i)** Which would you recommend they buy and why? Assume that the as the price increases the quality increases.

(ii) Will they save money in the long run? Show how you arrived at your answer.

After a few days Amy and Tom get bored with their layout. Uncle Richard has a large pile of bricks and about 10 two-metre lengths of guttering in his garage. He says they can use these to make their course more interesting.

(d) Make a new scale drawing of the crazy golf course using these extra materials.

Think about how long each hole needs to be – make some sketches first if necessary.

Technology

1   The table shows some information about broadband speeds
    in 2008.

ADSL speed	Typical download speed	Typical upload speed
512 kbps	460 kbps	200–240 kbps
1 Mbps	920 kbps	200–240 kbps
2 Mbps	1840 kbps	200–240 kbps
8 Mbps	7150 kbps	400–750 kbps

The ADSL speed is the maximum connection speed to the
internet.

1 kbps (kilobytes per second) = 1000 bytes per second

1 Mbps (Megabytes per second) = 1000 kbps

Download and upload speeds will vary due to traffic and
equipment. Figures shown are averages.

(a) How many bytes per second is 8 Mbps?

(b) Write the download speeds as Mbps.

(c) You want to download a film that has a size of 800 MB.
     How long will it take you to download the film at a speed of:

     (i) 250 kbps?   **(ii)** 460 kbps?   **(iii)** 920 kbps?

Give your answers in minutes and seconds.

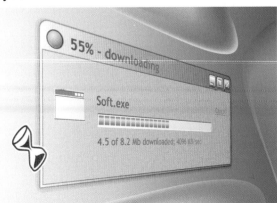

2 Mark wants to set up a formula in a spreadsheet.

	A	B	C	D	E
1					
2					
3					
4					

(a) He wants to take a value in cell A1 and add it to a value in cell B1, multiply by the value in cell C1 and put the result in cell E1. He writes down two formulae:

[Hint]

$$E1 = A1 + B1 * C1 \qquad E1 = (A1 + B1) * C1$$

Which formula is correct? Explain your answer.

(b) Work out the value of E for each of these formulae.

   (i) $E1 = A1 + B1 - C1$ $A1 = 3, B1 = 4, C1 = 2$

   (ii) $E1 = A1 + B1 - C1$ $A1 = 6, B1 = 3, C1 = 5$

   (iii) $E1 = A1 * B1 + C1$ $A1 = 4, B1 = 7, C1 = 3$

   (iv) $E1 = (A1 + B1 + C1) / 10$ $A1 = 5, B1 = 6, C1 = 9$

   (v) $E1 = 2 * A1 + B1 - C1$ $A1 = 7, B1 = 5, C1 = 4$

(c) Mark wants to find the average (mean) of A1, B1 and C1, and put the result in E1. Write down the formula he needs to use.

(d) The values in column D have been formatted to round numbers to a given number of decimal places.
Round the following numbers.

   (i) 4.3214 to 2 decimal places

   (ii) 5.00499 to 4 decimal places

   (iii) 0.5746 to 3 decimal places

   (iv) 0.0872 to 2 decimal places

   (v) 3.2314 to 1 decimal place

   (vi) 1.5296 to 3 decimal places

3   A computer controls two sets of disco lights.

| RED | BLUE | GREEN | YELLOW | | RED | BLUE | GREEN | YELLOW |

The simplest program is to have one light on from each set of lights. The computer selects the colour of the light to be shown at random.

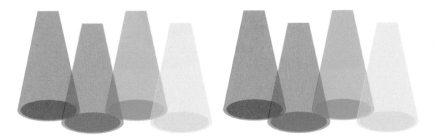

(a)   Write down all the possible combinations of colours that the computer could select.

Hint

(b)   Fred wanted to have 30 combinations, so he set the computer to select two lights from the first set and one from the second. Will this give the 30 combinations that he wanted?

4 Sarah is asked to gather information on household access to digital TV, internet and mobile phones in 2006. Her research assistant gave her the data like this.

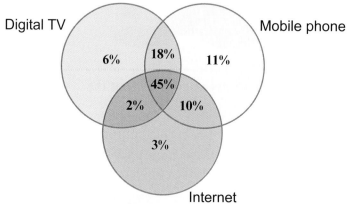

Digital TV — Mobile phone

6% 18% 11%

45%

2% 10%

3%

Internet

Sarah wants to convert the data into a table to summarise this information. Copy and complete her table.

Mobile phone	Internet	Digital TV	Percentage
✓	✗	✗	11%
✗	✓	✗	3%

5 Samuel carried out a survey into what internet users used the internet to do. This table shows his results.

Use	Percentage
Finding information about goods/services	82
Using email	80
General browsing	72
Information about travel and accommodation	70
Buying/ordering travel/goods/services	58
Personal banking	42
Reading news	36
Playing/downloading music	32
Selling goods/services	18

(a) Samuel decides to display this information as a graph in a report.

Draw a graph to show this information for Samuel's report.

Hint

(b) Samuel decides to write some ratios for the report.

(i) Write, as a ratio in its simplest form, the percentage for personal banking to the percentage for reading news.

(ii) From the information given in the table, write two other ratios that Samuel might choose to put in his report.

2000 people took part in the survey.

(c) How many of these people use the internet for:

(i) email?

(ii) buying and ordering?

(iii) selling?

(d) These figures do not add up to 100%. Explain why.

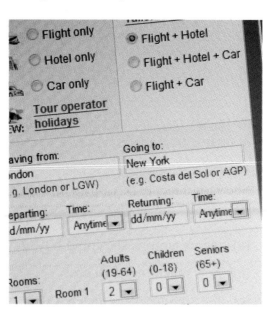

6 Hayley needs to order at least ten laptops for her staff. Here is a list of computers and specifications that have been recommended.

	Screen (inches)	Processor speed	RAM	Storage	Price
A	15.4	2 GHz	4096 MB	250 GB	£669.99
B	15.4	2.1 GHz	4096 MB	250 GB	£679.99
C	17	2 GHz	3072 MB	320 GB	£589.99
D	12	2.2 GHz	3072 MB	250 GB	£699.99
E	13	2.3 GHz	4096 MB	320 GB	£699.99
F	15.4	2 GHz	3072 MB	250 GB	£569.99
G	15	2.1 GHz	2048 MB	250 GB	£599.99
H	12	2.1 GHz	3072 MB	160 GB	£639.99

All the laptops need to have RAM of at least 3000 megabytes, and a processor speed of at least 2 gigahertz.

The storage capacity of at least four of the laptops needs to be 320 gigabytes, and for the remainder of the laptops it needs to be at least 250 gigabytes.

Hayley has a budget of £7000.
She would like to buy more than ten laptops for her staff.

Work out:

(a) which laptops she could buy

(b) how much they will cost

(c) the amount of money left over from the £7000.

Hint

7 These are the charges for two mobile phone networks.

Network Nation:
15p per minute for the first 5 minutes, then 5p per minute.

Keep in Touch:
15p per minute for the first 5 minutes, then 5 minutes free, then the remainder at 15p per minute.

(a) Calculate the cost of charges for a telephone call of these lengths for both networks.

   (i) 5 minutes   **(ii)** 10 minutes

   (iii) 15 minutes   **(iv)** 20 minutes

(b) After what period of time will Network Nation become cheaper than Keep in Touch?

   Hint

(c) Pimtel is choosing which network to sign up for. He guesses that he might make two or three 5 to 10 minute calls and one call of between 20 and 30 minutes each day.

Which network should he sign up for?
Justify your choice by showing your working and by explaining how you made your choice.

8 DIY PC

Make sure you write down all of your working and answers clearly.

Mia has just bought a new computer system.

The old system has an out-of-date processor, video and sound cards as well as a very small memory.

However, the case is usable, as are the motherboard, keyboard, speakers, monitor, DVD and hard drives.

There is also an up-to-date operating system loaded.

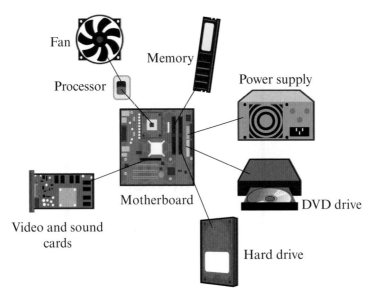

Amy, her younger sister, wants to update Mia's old system. She can easily remove the old components and slot new ones into their places on the motherboard.

She browses on the internet using Mia's new system to find some prices. Most computer magazines and websites give prices exclusive of VAT (ex. VAT).

Processor	Price (ex. VAT)	Speed
Pentium E2180	£44.80	2 GHz
Core 2 Duo E8600	£168.00	3.33 GHz
Core 2 Duo E6550	£106.40	2.33 GHz
Phenom X4 9750	£99.20	2.4 GHz
Phenom X3 8450	£57.60	2.1 GHz
Phenom II X4 940	£166.00	3 GHz

Video card	Price (ex. VAT)	Onboard memory
AT12-347	£56.99	256 MB
EVGA	£72.20	512 MB
6600-GT	£95.00	128 MB
980-GT	£89.06	512 MB

Sound card	Price (ex. VAT)	Notes
True sound	£31.97	Movie quality, loud and true
Soundforce 5.3	£14.10	TV quality sound
Soundmaker 7.1	£9.29	Basic economy card
Soundblaster	£33.74	Excellent, realistic quality audio
Klear as a bell	£23.50	Clear sound

Memory	Price (incl. VAT)	Notes
4GB P57-A	£62.50	4 GB
PC 250	£11.22	1 GB
DV7-2	£20.84	2 GB
DC 530	£10.93	1 GB
MMCX-1	£20.84	2 GB

Amy wants to recondition her 'new' computer for games and surfing the net.

This means she will need about 2 GB of memory, a fast processor of at least 3 GHz and a video card with at least 256 MB of onboard memory and a sound card.

(a) Mia says that Amy won't be able to recondition the old computer for less than £260. Is Mia right?
Support your answer with calculations and reasons.

VAT is $17\frac{1}{2}\%$.

(b) Amy has a friend check her motherboard. He says that there are enough slots to allow a lot more memory. He advises her to buy a total of 8 GB of memory.

Assuming there are enough memory slots on the motherboard, what is the cheapest way of doing this using the information in the tables?

(c) Amy enjoyed reconditioning the old computer. She downloaded an article about DIY PC building and made a note of all the other items she needs and their prices including VAT.

Could Amy build a basic PC for less than £400?

To build a basic PC, you will need at least

- Processor
- Memory
- Video card
- Sound card

- Keyboard & mouse about £20 on ebay
- PC case, cooling fan and power supply £65 special offer local shop
- Hard drive £35 mail order
- DVD drive £25 computer magazine
- Motherboard £80 best on-line price

(d) What, if any, is the connection between processor speed and cost?

Use the information in the tables to estimate the cost of a 4 GHz processor.

Yogurt

YALPine manufactures yogurt and produces it in small 150 g pots and large 450 g pots.

1 The label contains information about nutritional values.

The nutritional value per 100 g of YALPine yogurt is:

Energy	57 kilocalories
Protein	4.7 g
Carbohydrate	9.3 g
Fibre	1.0 g

(a) Work out the number of kilocalories in a 450 g pot of yogurt.

(b) Work out the protein in a 150 g pot of yogurt.

(c) What is the percentage of fibre in a 450 g pot of yogurt?

2 The design team tested four shapes of yogurt pot, A, B, C and D, each one filled with a different flavour of yogurt. Each pot has a different label. The design team carried out a survey, asking 20 people to put the four pots in order of preference for each factor.

The tables show how many people rated each of the four yogurt pots A, B, C and D. For example, three people put pot A in first place for shape and appearance.

Shape and appearance

	1st	2nd	3rd	4th
A	3	8	4	5
B	6	3	7	4
C	9	4	5	2
D	2	5	4	9

Information on label

	1st	2nd	3rd	4th
A	4	7	3	6
B	6	5	6	3
C	4	4	8	4
D	6	4	3	7

Flavour and taste

	1st	2nd	3rd	4th
A	7		6	4
B	8			4
C		6	1	
D	2	5		

(a) Copy and complete the table of results for flavour and taste.

(b) Which pot gained the most **(i)** 1st places **(ii)** 4th places overall?

(c) To judge the best pot in each category, points are given as follows: 5 points for each 1st place, 3 points for each 2nd place, 2 points for each 3rd place and 1 point for each 4th place.

Hint

   (i) Work out the total number of points for each pot for each of the three categories.

   (ii) Which pot scored most points overall?

   (iii) If the decision as to which pot is the best is based upon the number of 1st places, would the result have been the same?

(d) What advice would you give to YALPine, in terms of the type of pot, label and flavour?

3 The diagram shows a plan and front elevation of a yogurt pot.

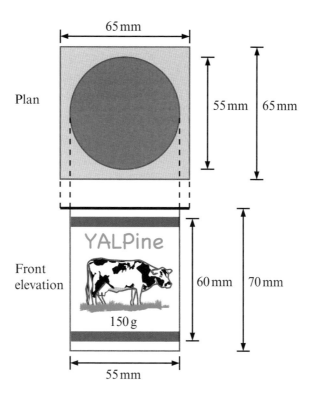

Plan

65 mm

55 mm | 65 mm

Front elevation

YALPine

150 g

60 mm | 70 mm

55 mm

(a) The top of a yogurt pot is covered with a square aluminium lid of side 65 mm. The lids are cut from aluminium sheets of dimensions 1 m by 60 cm.

Work out the maximum number of lids that can be cut from one of these aluminium sheets.

Hint

(b) Each pot is in the shape of a cylinder.

The label on a yogurt pot is made from a rectangular piece of paper of dimensions 175 mm by 60 mm.

By how many millimetres will the label overlap when wrapped around the yogurt pot?

Hint

(c) YALPine make a large container of yogurt which holds 400 litres of yogurt. This large container is used to fill some small pots of diameter $d = 55$ mm and height $h = 70$ mm.

Each pot is filled with yogurt to a level 5 mm from the top.

(i) Work out the volume of yogurt in each pot.
Give your answer correct to the nearest mm^3.

Hint

(ii) Work out how many small pots can be filled from the large container.

Note: 1 litre = 1 000 000 mm^3

117

4 (a) The yogurt pots in question **3** are packaged for sale.

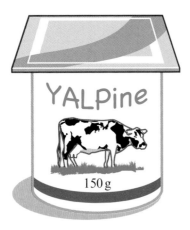

  (i) Fifty yogurt pots are packaged in packs of 4 and packs
      of 6. How many packs of 4 pots and packs of 6 pots
      can be packaged if there are no pots left over?

  (ii) Explain why 55 yogurt pots could not be packaged in
      packs of 4 and packs of 6 without any pots being left
      over.

  (iii) Sketch diagrams to show two different ways in which
      4 pots could be sensibly packaged together.

(b) Each pack of 4 pots is in the shape of a cuboid of
    dimensions 13 cm by 13 cm by 7 cm.
    Each pack of 6 pots is in the shape of a cuboid of
    dimensions 19.5 cm by 13 cm by 7 cm.

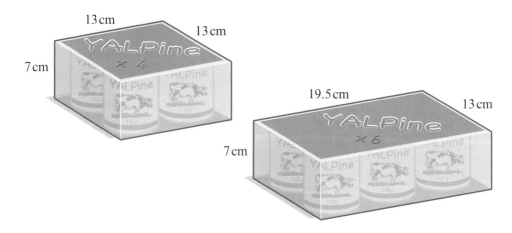

The packs are put into large boxes A, B and C, for distribution.

Which of the boxes below will hold the most yogurt pots if each box:

Hint

  (i) just contains packs of 4 pots

  (ii) just contains packs of 6 pots

(iii) contains a mixture of packs?

Note: yogurt pots must always be the right way up (lid at the top).

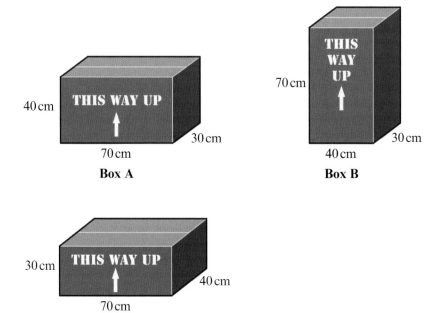

Box A

Box B

Box C

(c) YALPine decide to make their own boxes for distribution of the yogurt.

Design a box which will hold the 4 or 6 packs in it.
So that it is easy to carry, it should hold no more than 8 kg of yogurt. Remember: A small yogurt pot weighs 150 g.

  (i) Make a scale drawing of the net of the box.

(ii) Draw what it will look like as a 3-D drawing.

Note: yogurt pots must always be the right way up (lid at the top).

5 The flow chart shows the production process of YALPine yogurt.

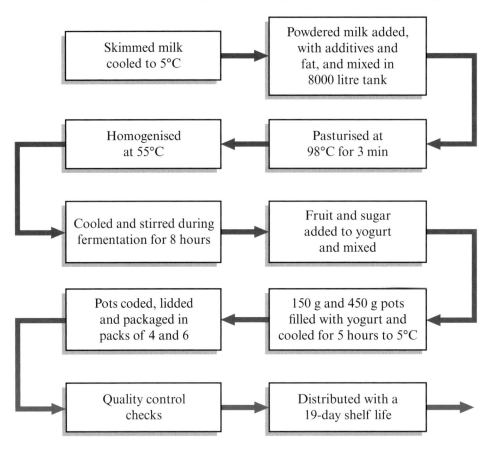

Skimmed milk cooled to 5°C	Powdered milk added, with additives and fat, and mixed in 8000 litre tank
Homogenised at 55°C	Pasturised at 98°C for 3 min
Cooled and stirred during fermentation for 8 hours	Fruit and sugar added to yogurt and mixed
Pots coded, lidded and packaged in packs of 4 and 6	150 g and 450 g pots filled with yogurt and cooled for 5 hours to 5°C
Quality control checks	Distributed with a 19-day shelf life

(a) The pots are filled by machines which can fill a batch of ten 150 g pots at the same time. The machine fills 8000 pots in one hour. Work out how many seconds it takes to fill a batch of ten 150 g pots.

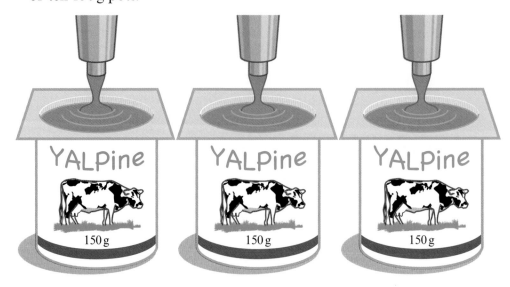

(b) From cooling the skimmed milk to filling the pots with yogurt takes 15 hours. The machines are then cleaned which takes no more than one hour.

Hint

(i) How many times in one week can these machines be used to produce yogurt ready for potting?

(ii) If each whole process (one run) produces 8000 litres of yogurt, how many litres of yogurt can be produced in one week?

(c) Sometimes it is found that the lids on the yogurt pots are not sealed. The pot is then thrown away. In one particular run, 52 000 pots were produced and 80 pots were thrown away because their lids were not sealed.

(i) What is the probability that a pot will be thrown away during quality control? Give your answer as a decimal correct to 4 decimal places.

(ii) Use the information in parts **(b)** and **(c)** to estimate how many pots are thrown away in one run where the same number of 150 g pots and 450 g pots are produced. A 150 g pot holds 70 ml of yogurt and a 450 g pot holds 210 ml of yogurt.

Hint

6 YALPine supplies five major stores:

Airdales (A), Bellum's (B), Choudry's (C), Dilip's (D) and Ellen's (E). The sketch shows the distances of these stores from YALPine's plant. (The distances are all in kilometres.)

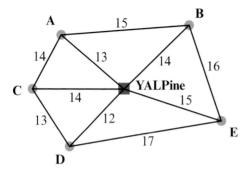

A large container van is used to supply the stores.
A van can carry no more than 500 boxes.
The number of boxes delivered to each store on one day is:

store A = 150 boxes, store B = 300 boxes, store C = 250 boxes, store D = 175 boxes and store E = 225 boxes.

(a) Work out the order in which the van could supply all of the stores, returning to refill the least number of times.

(b) Work out the least distance the van needs to travel to complete the deliveries to all of the stores. The van does not need to return to YALPine after the last delivery.

Hint

7 Making Yogurt

YALPine also produce probiotic yogurt and want to take a fresh look at the flavours of yogurt they produce.

One hundred of YALPine's customers were asked to put yogurt flavours in order of preference. The flavours tested were cherry, blueberry, strawberry and raspberry. The results are given in the table.

Flavour	Position			
	1st	2nd	3rd	4th
Blueberry	11	39	13	37
Cherry	33	17	21	29
Raspberry	27	14	49	10
Strawberry	29	30	17	24

The probiotic yogurt is produced in 125 g pots. The pots are sold in packs of six.

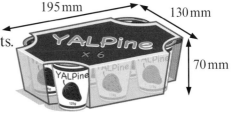

The packs measure 195 mm by 130 mm and are 70 mm high.

Yogurt is delivered each day. YALPine has just bought a new van. This is its specification.

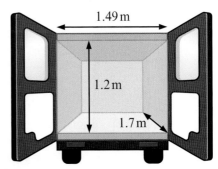

Dimensions of van space	1.7 m L × 1.49 m W × 1.2 m H
Maximum weight that can be carried	600 kg
Typical fuel consumpton (mpg)	33

Make sure you write down all of your working and answers clearly.

(a) Jasmine and other members of the team disagree over which is the most popular yogurt flavour.

    (i) Tony says that over 50% of people chose either raspberry or strawberry as their first choice. Is he correct?

    Explain how you arrived at your answer.

    (ii) Andy says that cherry is the most popular flavour because more people chose this as their first choice. But Jasmine says that blueberry did much better as second choice.

    Find a better and fairer way of deciding which is the most popular yogurt flavour.

    Use your method to put the flavours in order of their popularity.

(b) YALPine produces about 1000 packs of probiotic yogurt a day.

Use your working and answers to part **(a) (ii)** to estimate how many pots of each flavour they should produce.

(c) Yoghurts are packed into boxes with three layers of four packs in each box.

    (i) Work out the dimensions of the boxes.

    (ii) What is the maximum number of boxes can the van hold? Remember that boxes must remain upright.

(iii) The largest order Andy has to deliver to any one store is 300 packs. The packs are put into boxes. It takes Andy about 4 minutes to carry a load of packs from the van to the storeroom, put them on the shelves and walk back to the van.

How long will it take him to unload the 300 packs?
Jot down any assumptions that you make and make sure that someone else can understand your working. Andy is quite fit – but he isn't the world's strongest man!

(d) Thursday is a busy day for Andy. He has to deliver to five large stores. All need 240 packs. The round trip to these stores and back is 120 km.

Andy wants to know long he can expect to be working that day.
On average it takes about an hour to load the van at YALPine
and about 45 minutes to unload and complete the paperwork at each store.
The average speed of the van is about 50 km/h.
Andy starts work at 8 a.m. and has a one hour lunch break.

He jotted down these word formulae to help him.

$$speed = \frac{distance}{time}$$

$$time = \frac{distance}{speed}$$

$$distance = speed \times time$$

What is the earliest time he could arrive back at YALPine after making all five deliveries?

Oil

1 An oil company has two refineries: refinery A and refinery B.

The cost of operating refinery A for one day is £10 000.

Each day it produces 100 barrels of high-grade oil and 300 barrels of low-grade oil.

The cost of operating refinery B for one day is £9000.

Each day it produces 200 barrels of high-grade oil and 200 barrels of low-grade oil.

An order is received for 2000 barrels of high-grade oil and 3600 barrels of low-grade oil.

For how many days should each refinery operate to fill the order at the lowest cost? What is the lowest cost?

2 The scale diagram below gives information about the locations of five oil rigs.

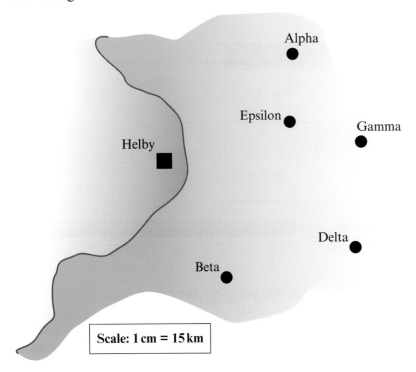

A helicopter visits all of these oil rigs to collect and deliver mail. It starts and finishes its journey at Helby. The helicopter flies at an average speed of 90 km/h. At each oil rig, it takes 8 minutes to land and 15 minutes to collect and deliver the mail. The helicopter leaves Helby at 09 00.

Work out a schedule for the helicopter.

Hint

3 An engineer needs some pipes cut to particular lengths.

This table gives information about the lengths and the numbers of pipes the engineer needs.

Length (m)	Number
2	4
3	2
4	6
5	4
8	3

The engineer has a number of 12 m pipes from which these smaller pipes must be cut.

12 m

Show how this can be done so that the engineer uses the lowest number of 12 m pipes.

4 This diagram shows the pipes connecting five storage containers. The numbers in the diagram represent the lengths, in metres, of the pipes.

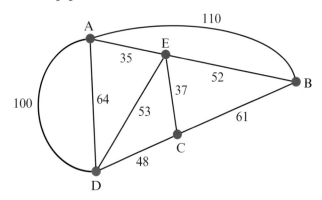

An engineer walks along the lengths of the pipes and inspects them for damage.

(a) Does it matter which route the engineer takes if he must start and end at B. Explain you answer.

Hint

The time taken to investigate each length of pipe is directly proportional to the length of that pipe. It takes the engineer 30–40 seconds to inspect 8 metres of pipe.

(b) How long will it take the engineer to inspect all the pipes?

5 On oil rigs, helicopters land on a helipad.

Here is a diagram of a helipad. It shows a circle drawn inside a square. The side of the square has length 15 m.

This helipad is painted with two types of paint.

The shaded region in the diagram is painted with Polyplus paint, and the circular region is painted with Turbocarb paint.

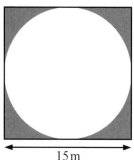

15 m

The shaded region needs two coats of paint.

5 litres of paint covers about 20 square metres.

This table shows the sizes and costs of tins of the two types of paint.

	5 litres	10 litres	20 litres
Turbocarb	£157	£276	£493
Polyplus	£75	£120	£215

Work out the cheapest cost for painting the helipad. Give your answer to the nearest pound.

Write down which size tin you would choose for each type of paint and show your working.

Hint

THIS WEEK'S SPECIAL

Buy 2 10-litre cans of Turbocarb and get **10% discount**.

Buy 2 10-litre cans of Polyplus and get **20% discount**.

6 A standard barrel of oil
contains 159 litres of oil.

Hint

(a) Design a cylindrical container for a standard barrel of
oil. The height, h, of your cylindrical container should be
between two and three times the diameter, d.

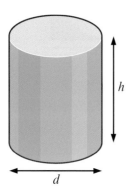

The mass of $1\,m^3$ of oil is $900\,kg$.

(b) Work out the mass of oil in a standard barrel.

Hint

Your cylindrical oil container is rolled $25\,m$ from a warehouse to
a truck.

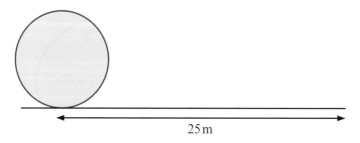

25 m

(c) Through how many turns will it roll?

Hint

7 Oil spillage at sea

Make sure you write down all of your working and answers clearly.

Most of the world's oil is transported by sea in oil tankers.

Sometimes there are accidents and oil is spilt in the sea.

Oil facts

An average oil slick has a thickness of about 0.1 mm.

On average, 1 kg of oil has a volume of $0.0011 \, m^3$.

$1 \, m^3$ of oil has, on average, a mass of 900 kg.

Amounts of oil are measured in standard barrels.

A standard barrel contains 159 litres (or $0.159 \, m^3$).

Tanker facts

A super tanker can hold as much as 500 000 tonnes of oil.

(1 tonne is 1000 kg.)

Earth facts

The total surface area of the Earth is $510 000 000 \, km^2$.

About 70% of the Earth's surface is covered by sea.

These tables show figures published by The International Tanker Owners Pollution Federation Ltd.

Year	Number of spills		Annual spillage (tonnes)
	7 to 700 tonnes	More than 700 tonnes	
1990	51	14	61 000
1991	29	7	430 000
1992	31	10	172 000
1993	31	11	139 000
1994	26	9	130 000
1995	20	3	12 000
1996	20	3	80 000
1997	28	10	72 000
1998	25	5	13 000
1999	19	6	29 000
2000	19	4	14 000
2001	16	3	8 000
2002	12	3	67 000
2003	15	4	42 000
2004	16	5	15 000
2005	21	3	17 000
2006	11	4	13 000
2007	10	4	18 000
2008	7	1	2 000

These are the worst oil spillages between 1990 and 2008.

Year	Ship	Nearest country	Spill size (tonnes)
1991	ABT Summer	Angola	260 000
1991	Haven	Italy	144 000
1993	Braer	UK	85 000
1992	Aegean Sea	Spain	74 000
1996	Sea Empress	UK	72 000
1992	Katina P	Mozambique	72 000
2002	Prestique	Spain	63 000

Jake had a look at this data and came to two conclusions.

Claim 1

Just one super tanker sinking and releasing all its oil could cover half the sea on Earth with a layer of oil.

Claim 2

In fact oil spills are getting less and are becoming less frequent.

Is Jake right? Use the information to investigate both of his claims. Show how you arrived at your conclusions.

Trains

1 This is part of the timetable for trains from Manchester to London.

Manchester Piccadilly	0602	0645	0715	0745	0805
Stockport	0611	0653	0723	0755	
Macclesfield	0624	0709	0737	0807	
Stoke-on-Trent	0640	0724	0753	0822	
Watford Junction	0802	0842	0920	0944	
London Euston	0827	0907	0945	1009	

(a) How long does it take to get from Watford Junction to London Euston?

Hint

(b) You want the fastest train from Manchester to London.

Which train should you catch?

Hint

(c) The 06 53 from Stockport is delayed and does not arrive in Macclesfield until 07 26.

At what time is it now likely to arrive at London Euston?

(d) The next train after the 07 45 is the 08 05.

Fill in the train times for the 08 05. It takes the same time between stations as the previous train.

(e) After this train, the trains run every 55 minutes until 20 00.

When do trains leave Manchester between 13 00 and 15 00?

(f) Draw up a table to show Manchester departure times from 08 05 to 20 00 and the London arrival times.

Which trains arrive in London after 16 00?

(g) It takes 30 minutes for a train to be cleaned and loaded ready for another journey.

How many trips can one train make to London and back if it needs to be back in Manchester before 23 00?

(h) The first train leaves Manchester at 06 02 and the last train leaves at 20 00. To run the timetable how many trains are needed to make all the trips between Manchester and London in one day?

Hint

(i) Anita needs to make a business trip from Manchester to London.

Her meeting is at 14 30. She needs to allow about 20 minutes to get a taxi from the station to the meeting. After the meeting, which should take 3 hours, she needs to travel back to Manchester.

Which train should Anita catch to go to the meeting?

When is she likely to get back to Manchester?

2 This is a plan of a train carriage.

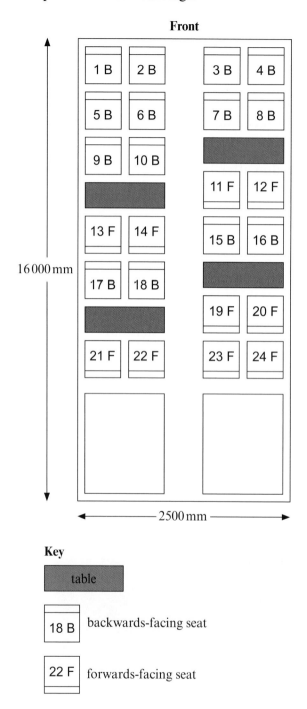

(a) A carriage has a length of 16 000 mm and a width of 2500 mm.

Convert these measurements into metres.

(b) What is the area of the floor of the train carriage in m²?

Hint

(c) Bob has been asked to lay carpet in one of the train carriages. The carpet is 2 m wide.

He could lay it lengthwise or widthwise. Sketch the best way Bob could lay the strips of carpet.

(d) How many metres of carpet are needed?

(e) A complete train has nine carriages.

There are 12 **pairs** of seats in each carriage.

John, the ticket inspector, is expecting the train to be about 80% full.

How many tickets is he expecting to collect on his travel through the train?

3 You are arranging a journey for eight people.
The table below shows their preferences and the diagram shows some seat numbers around a table in one of the carriages.

Name	Seat preference	Seat number
Ali	Forward	
Bahavana	Backwards	
Charlie	Either	
Kate	Either	
Ed	Forward	
Frank	Forward	
Gary	Backwards	
Heena	Either	

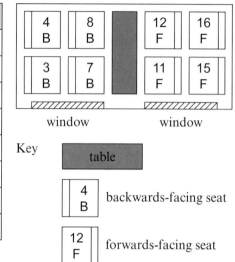

Key

(a) Ali, Bhavana, Charlie and Kate want to sit together at a table.

Kate and Charlie want to sit opposite each other.

Bahavana, Ed and Heena want window seats.

Copy and complete the table, showing the seat number you would give to each of them.

(b) Mark is given a seat at random in another carriage which is identical to the one shown in question **2**.
What is the probability that he is given a seat that faces forward and is not at a table?

[Hint]

4 Abida is travelling from London to Northallerton. The train takes $2\frac{1}{4}$ hours to travel between London and Northallerton. Abida estimates that it is about 225 miles from London to Northallerton.

Estimate the average speed of the train.

[Hint]

5 The graph shows the punctuality of trains over a two-year period.
It shows the percentage of trains that arrived on time each month.

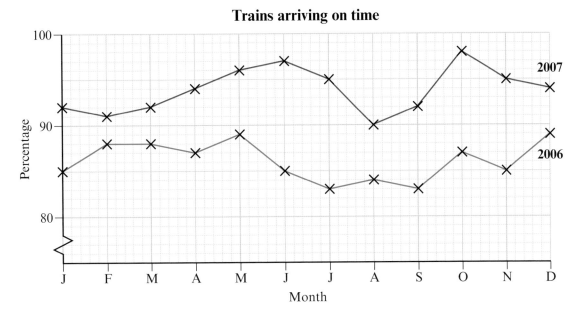

Trains arriving on time

(a) During how many months in 2006 were less than 85% of
trains on time?

(b) Make two comparisons between the graphs for 2006 and 2007.

(c) Calculate the mean percentages for (i) 2006 (ii) 2007. ⌈ Hint ⌉

(d) What is the range in punctuality percentages for
(i) 2006 (ii) 2007? ⌈ Hint ⌉

(e) There are 35 trains to London on a weekday.
On one day, 20% of trains were late.
How many trains were late?

(f) In a different week, engineering works were taking place on
Friday and Saturday. The table shows how many trains were
on time, and how many were late.

	On time	Late
Friday	21	14
Saturday	18	13

On which day was a greater proportion of trains late? ⌈ Hint ⌉
Give reasons for your answer.

6 There are two classes of train travel, standard and first.

A train company uses these formulae to work out the cost of first class tickets.

Monday to Friday: first class price = standard class price × 1.6

Saturday and Sunday: first class price = standard class price × 1.25

(a) A journey on a Saturday in standard class costs £36.

Work out the cost of a first class ticket.

(b) Ben has paid £128 for a first class ticket to travel on Friday.

How much less would a standard class ticket have cost?

(c) Patricia and her family want to buy a family railcard.

Family Railcard

ONLY £20

All adults (up to 4) $\frac{1}{3}$ off every trip

All children (up to 4) **60% off every trip**

There are four people in the family, two adults and two children.

They decide to travel to see a football match in Newcastle.

One adult return ticket is £25 full price.

All child fares are 50% of adult fares.

(i) If they buy a railcard and use it, do they save the £20 which the card cost or do they need to use it again before they make their money back?

Hint

(ii) Write two formulae to help Patricia work out the cost of the reduced fares for her family: one for each adult fare and one for each child fare.

Hint

7 Ahmed wants to travel to Gatwick Airport. He needs to catch a train from Manchester to London Euston, then catch another train from London Victoria to Gatwick Airport. Train times are shown in the tables.

Manchester Picadilly	1255	1315	1335	1355	1415	1435	1455	1515	1535
London Euston	1508	1528	1548	1608	1628	1648	1708	1728	1748

Allow 30 minutes to transfer from London Euston to London Victoria.

London Victoria	1515	1550	1625	1700	1735	1810	1845	1920	1955
Gatwick Airport	1545	1620	1655	1730	1805	1840	1915	1950	2025

(a) For Ahmed to catch his plane at Gatwick Airport he needs to arrive at 1830. Which train should he take from Manchester to make sure that he catches his plane?

(b) Fiona wants to catch the next train from London Victoria to Gatwick Airport. She looks at her watch. It is twenty to seven in the evening. Which train will she catch?

Hint

(c) I need to catch a train after 2 p.m. from Manchester to London. List the trains I could take.

(d) The 1415 train from Manchester is now running 17 minutes late. What is the earliest time that I can arrive at Gatwick Airport?

(e) If the pattern in train times carries on, how many more trains will leave from London Victoria for Gatwick Airport before midnight?

(f) Frankie is to catch a flight leaving Gatwick at 2005.
It is an international flight and so he has to be at the airport at least 2 hours before his flight.
Which trains from Manchester could he take to be sure of catching his flight?

8   Italian Getaway

Use the following information to plan a one week holiday in Italy for a family of five, Mum, Dad, Helen (aged 15), Sophie (aged 12) and Henry (aged 6). They will travel from Manchester and need to be at Gatwick Airport by 2000. They have a family railcard already. They also have a family car.

RETURN RAIL FARE

Adult fare: £43.20

All child fares are 50% of adult fares

Child is under 16

Family Railcard

ONLY £20

All adults (up to 4) $\frac{1}{3}$ **off every trip**

All children (up to 4)   **60% off every trip**

Manchester Picadilly	1355	1415	1435	1455	1515	1535	1555
London Euston	1608	1628	1648	1708	1728	1748	1808

Allow 30 minutes to transfer from London Euston to London Victoria.

London Victoria	1625	1700	1735	1810	1845	1925
Gatwick Airport	1655	1730	1805	1840	1915	1955

MANCHESTER TO LONDON
APPROX. 270 km

The family car travels 14 km per litre

Average cost per litre of petrol 90p

50 mph is about 80 km/h.

AIRPORT PARKING

Park your car in secure compound

Prices: £4.99 per day

(a) Work out possible travel arrangements for the family to and from the airport, including how long the journey takes. Compare lengths of time for the train journey and the car journey. Their average speed on long car journeys is 50 mph and they live next to the railway station.

(b) Work out the cost of travel to the airport.
Which mode of transport should they use? Give a reason for your choice.

Acknowledgements

Cover images l-r: ©Alehnia/Shutterstock, © Tony Watson Collection/Alamy, © Matt Cardy/Alamy, © Sculpies/Shutterstock, © BL Images Ltd/Alamy, © Beaucroft/Shutterstock

Photos on the following pages are from Alamy: p. 3 John Robertson; p. 6 Tony French; p. 13. Digital Vision; p. 19 Vario Images GmbH & Co. KG; p. 20 David Martin Hughes; p. 22, 33*tr* David R. Frazier Photolibrary Inc; p. 24 Clynt Garnham; p. 27 Jochen Tack; p.28 Photofusion Picture Library; p. 31, 46 Janine Wiedel Photolibrary; p. 33*tl* Rosemary Roberts; p. 33*b* PBimages; p. 42 Jeffrey Blackler; p. 50 David Hoffman Photo Library; p. 53 Aardvark; p. 54*t* Roger Bamber; p. 57 Adrian Sherratt; p. 59 Mediablitzimages (UK) Limited; p. 66, 96 Kim Karpeles; p. 68, 75*t* PhotoStock-Israel; p. 70 Alex Segre; p. 71 Rob Marmion; p. 72 Images Ect Ltd; p. 74 Adi; p. 75*b* Faiz Balabil; p. 70 Interfoto; p. 87 Islemount Images; p. 101 Doug Houghton; p. 109 Steven May; p. 115 Nigel Cattlin; p. 116 Tetra Images; p. 121 RIA Novosti; p. 123 Vibrant Image Studio; p. 134 Phil Grain; p. 135 Jonathan Larsen; p. 137 Alberto Paredes; p. 142 Colin Palmer Photography; p. 143 Travelshots.com

Photos on the following pages are from Shutterstock: p. 2 Tan Kian Khoon; p. 5 Pitroviz; p. 8 Kevin Renes; p. 10 dwphotos; p. 11 Losevsky Pavel; p. 17 Elena Elisseeva; p. 36 Daniel Goodchild; p. 38 WizData Inc.; p. 39 Michael Zysman; p. 41 Ieva Geneviciene; p. 52 R. Nagy; p. 54*b* Monkey Business Images; p. 62 Andrey Armyagov; p. 65 Nata Sdobnikova; p. 81 Mikael Damkier; p. 90 Brasiliao; p. 91 El Greco; p. 97 Taylor Jackson; p. 98 LWPhotography; p. 99 Rozilynn Mitchell; p. 105 Artem Efimov; p. 107 Vadim Kozlovsky; p. 108 Yuri Arcurs; p. 110 Karen Struthers; p. 111 Gabor Radvanyi; p. 126 Johannes Compaan; p. 127 Tonylady; p. 129 Manuel; p. 130 Stephen Sweet; p. 132 Andy Z.

Photos on the following pages are from Jupiter Images: p. 45, 125, 138